Fishy·Fishy

COOKBOOK

KT-376-931

In memory of Richard Rumball

Published in 2011 by New Holland Publishers (UK) Ltd
London • Cape Town • Sydney • Auckland
www.newhollandpublishers.com

Garfield House, 86–88 Edgware Road, London W2 2EA
United Kingdom

80 McKenzie Street, Cape Town 8001, South Africa
Unit 1, 66 Gibbes Street, Chatswood, NSW 2067, Australia
218 Lake Road, Northcote, Auckland, New Zealand

Text copyright © 2011 James Ginzler, Paul Shovlin and Loz Talent
Photography copyright © New Holland Publishers (UK) Ltd, except
those listed on page 192
Copyright © 2011 New Holland Publishers (UK) Ltd

James Ginzler, Paul Shovlin and Loz Talent have asserted their moral
right to be identified as the authors of this work.

All rights reserved. No part of this publication may be reproduced,
stored in any retrieval system or transmitted, in any form or by
any means, electronic, mechanical, photocopying, recording or
otherwise, without the prior written permission of the publishers
and copyright holders.

A catalogue record for this book is available from the British Library.

ISBN 978 184773 819 6

Publisher: Clare Sayer
Consultant editor: Robert Johnston
Designer: Geoff Borin (www.geoffborin.com)
Photographer: Tony Briscoe
Additional photography: Hazel Thompson
Production Controller: Laurence Poos
Fishy Fishy is supported by Atlantic Swiss

10 9 8 7 6 5 4 3 2 1

Reproduction by PDQ Digital Media Solutions Ltd, United Kingdom
Printed and bound in Singapore by Tien Wah Press PTE Ltd

CPO

Please return / renew by date shown.
You can renew at: **norlink.norfolk.gov.uk**
or by telephone: **0344 800 8006**
Please have your library card & PIN ready.

SPECIAL LOAN

641.692

NORFOLK LIBRARY
AND INFORMATION SERVICE

NORFOLK ITEM

30129 068 007 351

Fishy·Fishy

COOKBOOK

James Ginzler, Paul Shovlin & Loz Talent

Foreword by Dermot O'Leary

NH
NEW
HOLLAND

Contents

Foreword

I turn the corner and see the tables and blue umbrellas in the cobbled square, hear the murmur of contented punters and the clinking of glasses suggesting that just one more glass could be squeezed in before the sun sets, and breathe in the smell of the sea drifting up East Street, as well as the delicious aromas coming from our restaurant kitchen. I get butterflies as I descend the steps as quickly as possible to find the usual chaos of a kitchen in the middle of service. I'm always fascinated to discover what has been brought in that morning and to see what magic Loz and his kitchen staff have worked on the day's catch.

From the very outset, all of us involved in setting up Fishy Fishy – Paul, James, our better halves Alice and Dee and I – made it absolutely clear that the kitchen had to be the heartbeat of the restaurant. Before anything else was confirmed (including, I recall, the funding!), we were making sure our chef Loz was busy creating a superb menu, with an awful lot of unnecessary help from us five clucking hens. We wanted something that reflected the best Brighton and the Channel has to offer, a feat we've since repeated with heartfelt passion in our second restaurant in Poole.

The idea is simple. Well, that's it exactly, simplicity. We have an incredible larder right on our doorstep, which if fished and managed correctly, can provide us with a varied and delicious menu. I really don't think that the words 'local' and 'seasonal' are mere fads – our parents and grandparents (in fact everyone before them) always bought their food this way. Or course they didn't have as much choice as we do now and you were unlikely to find exotic fish flown half way across the world in your local supermarket half a century ago. But we do have a choice now and buying local produce, in season is both the right and tastiest thing to do.

It's what we, the Fishy Fishy 'family', all passionately believe in, as important as the way the place looks and feels, the welcome you receive, the pleasure you get from what's on your plate and what's in your glass.

We really hope you enjoy these recipes – many of these are dishes straight off our menu but we've included others from further afield. And perhaps you might come and pay us a visit...

Dermot O'Leary

Introduction

Back in 1946, *Animal Farm* author George Orwell wrote an essay in the *London Evening Standard* about his perfect pub, The Moon Under Water. This was a place where the whole was so much better than its parts. Other places might do particular bits better, but no one offered such a perfect package.

   Through my work I have eaten in countless different eateries around the world, from palatial places in Paris with three Michelin stars, to back-street pizzerias in Milan. And believe me, very few have come anywhere near perfection. So when I was first asked to be involved in Fishy Fishy I felt that here was the restaurant world's answer to Orwell's fictitious hostelry – somewhere just around the corner that you could eat at once a week, if you so wished, as well as a destination restaurant you would make the effort to visit. A place where you could have a quick bite – because you couldn't be bothered to cook that night – or really push the boat out for a special celebration. I am happy to say that I was right and that the Fishy Fishy team has achieved this balance brilliantly.

   At home I have shelves full of cookbooks, but very few of them live up to their expectations, so I'm delighted with the book that the Fishy Fishy team has produced. In the same way that I want to eat every dish on the Fishy Fishy menu, I want to cook and eat every recipe in this book. Inspired by the restaurant's menu, you can recreate some fantastic dishes, from quick healthy suppers to lobster feasts that would make any occasion a celebration, to simple and delicious food with which to impress your friends. It is designed to be a book you will open and enjoy again and again. So go on, push the fishing boat out.

Robert Johnston
Associate Editor, GQ Magazine

8

The Fishy Fishy ethos

It's always been pretty straightforward: fresh, local, seasonal fish and shellfish caught in the most environmentally friendly and sustainable way.

Fresh

The freezer has had a dramatic effect on the supply of fish and shellfish from far-flung corners of the globe. You can pretty much buy any fish from around the world at any time. A boat can fish in deep seas with huge nets for weeks on end. It can hoover up whole shoals and sort, fillet and freeze until it's bursting from the seams before returning to port to sell its catch to the manufacturers of fish fingers and frozen fish pies. And while this may mean that we can fill our freezers with cheap fish, the real cost, apart from the obvious damage to the ocean's fish stocks, is to the taste.

Fresh fish, caught in the least damaging way possible (both to the fish and the sea) using a hook and line, or tidal nets, transported back to port and sold the same day, simply has a superior taste to anything you can find in the frozen food section. Fresh fish does not smell of fish, it smells of the sea and this flavour flows through the body to the fillet.

Our fish and shellfish are delivered fresh every day, sometimes twice a day and, in the case of our shellfish, still alive. This is not because we buy in particularly large quantities, it's because we want our suppliers to deliver the freshest fish possible. So when you are next at the fishmongers or standing at the fish counter at your local supermarket, just ask a simple question: is it fresh? If the answer is no, then go elsewhere.

Local

Here in the United Kingdom we celebrate the fact that we are an island, surrounded by sea which contains a fantastic assortment of fish and shellfish. So why do we fly thousands of tonnes of fish into this country from around the world? Lobsters from Maine, prawns from Indonesia, farmed bream and sea bass from Greece and even green-lipped mussels from New Zealand. Most consumers have never been to these places so why are we offered food from there when we have perfectly good alternatives here in the UK? The UK mussel industry has taken great steps towards producing grit-free, organic mussels. Most towns have at least one fishmonger who can source alternatives to these exotic specimens, either from the local fishing fleet or from the bigger fish markets. And you'll be surprised how little they can cost.

Seasonal

When we started to look at what we were going to serve at Fishy Fishy, the seasonal availability of fish and shellfish did take us by surprise. It seems obvious to us now but the types of fish available vary enormously depending on how warm or cold the sea water is. We are all so used to eating strawberries at Christmas or lobster on New Year's Eve that we never really think about when food is actually in season and, therefore, at its best. So if you want to save money while still enjoying good-quality fish, think carefully about what's in season – you can usually always find a suitable alternative (see the chart on page 187).

During the hot summer months our thoughts turn to sitting outside with a nice cold glass of Sauvignon Blanc and maybe some mackerel or Cornish sardines spitting away over the hot coals of a barbecue. And what could be better than tucking into a cold crab or lobster with crisp French fries, or dunking deep-fried calamari into freshly made garlic mayonnaise? Well it turns out all these are available in plentiful supply across the summer months. So they are not going to cost the earth.

In winter lobsters and sea bass disappear to find calmer, warmer waters while the white fish return with the colder seas. Cod, pollock, hake and whiting all make an appearance and before you know it, it's scallop season. You should avoid some flat fish in mid-winter when they are spawning but they are still around. So if you want to eat lobster in the middle of winter it's probably going to be flown in from Canada and it will cost a lot more money.

If you really want fresh, local fish and shellfish you are going to have to accept that you can't have it all, all of the time. But what you will have will be of the best quality, probably not cost the earth and taste great. For me there's nothing better than looking forward to that first line-caught mackerel of the summer or rediscovering fresh scallops pan-fried with a little garlic butter on a cold winter night.

Controls and quotas

If you eat fish you will have undoubtedly realized that you need to ask questions about how your fish is caught. There is no doubt that there are areas of the fishing industry which are taking too much fish and shellfish from the seas with little or no thought of future stocks. Each year another fish is highlighted by the environmentalists as being in serious threat, whether it's the prized blue-fin tuna or the humble cod. But there is a future for commercial farming and as a consumer you are in the best position to lead it.

So where do you start? Firstly in the UK and Europe there is a generally agreed understanding that fishing has to be controlled. This is done with quotas, where a set tonnage of fish that can be taken from each part of the sea is allocated across a period of time. This is enforced here in Britain by the Marine and Fisheries Agency who monitor what the commercial fishermen are doing. Every fish caught in British waters is logged and its size and condition recorded. Therefore it is possible to trace every fish served to you back to where and how it was caught. Obviously there are some fishermen who don't record their catch and sell them on the black market, this 'black' fish is not monitored and obviously can't be traced. So when you buy fish you should be able to ask how and when it was caught and with what method. If you don't get an answer then it's probably best to go elsewhere.

13

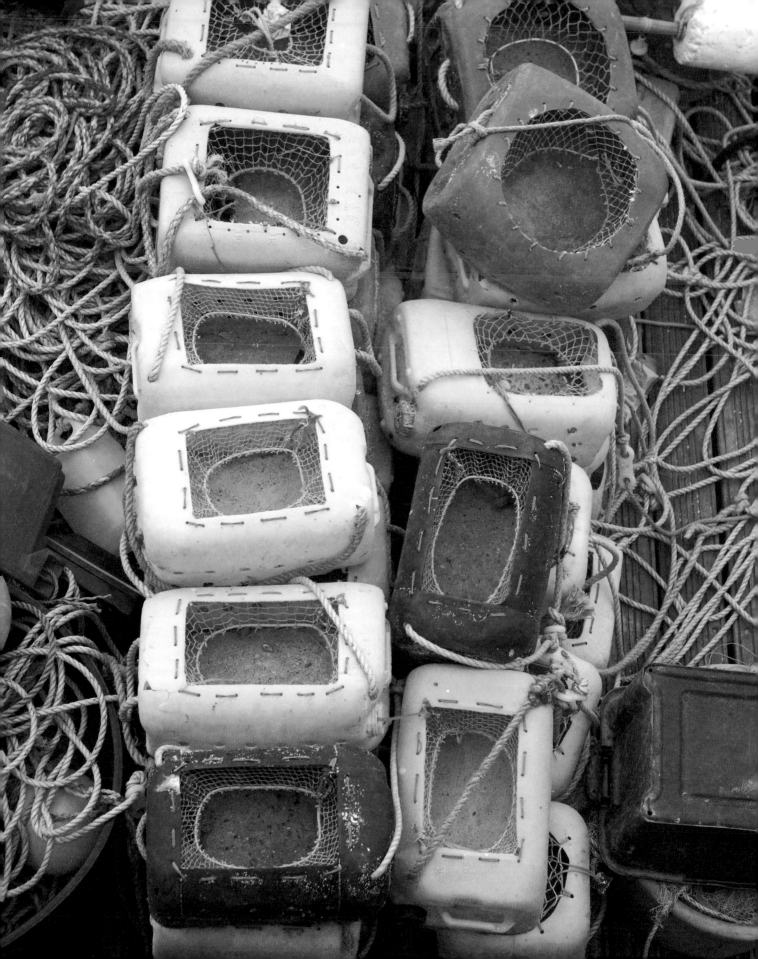

Fishing methods

There are three main ways fish are caught commercially. Towed gear or nets, encircling gear and static gear. The size of the boat and the amount it can catch is determined by the method it uses and the type of fish they are after.

Towed gear

Towing a large net behind a fishing boat is the oldest and most common method of catching fish. A boat simply pulls one or two large nets behind it, either across the seabed (beam trawling) or at a set depth (bottom trawling). Beam trawling is used to target bottom-feeding fish like plaice, Dover sole and, in deeper waters, monkfish and prawns. Bottom trawling, where the net is pulled above the seabed, targets shoals of mackerel, sea bass, cod, haddock and whiting. Bottom dredging is also used to catch scallops, where the boat drags a metal mesh with a net behind it across the ground. This forces the scallops in the sand to jump up into the water; they are then caught in the nets behind.

Fishermen use sonar equipment as well as their own knowledge to target large shoals of a specific fish, but in the process they can't help but pull in other species. If there is no quota for these fish they have to be thrown back into the sea. There are controls on the size of the nets the boats can use and the size of the holes in the net to allow smaller fish to escape. These boats will often be at sea for a few days, selecting, cleaning and storing their catch in ice before sailing back to the fish markets when they are full.

Encircling gear

As the name suggests, this is where the fishing boat surrounds a shoal of fish with a long-line net which will scoop the fish out of the water. This is a very skilled way of catching fish and the fishermen have to find large shoals of fast-moving fish like mackerel, sardine, herring and, in warmer waters, tuna. They then surround this moving group of fish with a net before pulling them in. They can be very specific about what fish they are targeting and this method does not cause any damage to the seabed. The downside is that they can't really limit the size of each fish. Modern trawlers don't even bring the nets on board but simply suck the fish out of the water once they are close to the surface and store them still alive in giant chilled sea water tanks and then head quickly back to port when they are full.

Static gear

This covers a variety of different methods to catch fish and shellfish and are most often used by smaller day boats which leave and return to port each day. In each case the gear used to catch the fish are left static on the seabed or floating above it and only catch fish which stray into them. The size of the fish can be determined by the size of the holes in the net which means smaller fish simply swim through. Also, by using floats and weights,

15

the amount of time the gear is actively catching fish can be controlled.

Gill nets are so called because they catch the fish by the gills as they try and swim through them. They are rectangular in shape and hang like a curtain. They can be anchored to the ground or in some cases, allowed to float on the surface of the water while attached to the boat.

Hook and line is an even more specific method of catching fish as the size of the fish can be determined by the hook and the bait used. The fisherman simply lets out lines of anything up to a mile or more of baited hooks and waits for the fish to take the bait. Fish caught in this way can demand a higher premium at market as they are considered to be in the best condition. Again, there is very little damage to the seabed unless the line becomes caught and, as the fish have the advantage, it is often considered the most sustainable way of fishing.

Pots and creels

Lobster, crabs, whelks and cuttlefish are nearly all caught using static pots laid to rest on the sea floor. They are often baited with unwanted or unsellable catch from other

fishing methods which attract the scavengers into their underwater prison. The pots are often left for a day or so to maximize the chances of actually catching anything as the shellfish are quite able to survive in the trap, unless there is another one in the same trap and they try and eat each other. Once the traps are brought to the surface the catch is measured, with any undersize thrown back for another day. Lobsters have their claws bound to stop them injuring anyone with a nasty nip, while crabs are crippled by cutting through the tendons. The shellfish are then brought to shore and often kept in seawater tanks to be sold live.

Farming

Increasingly fish farming is leading the way in reducing the demands on the sea for wild-caught fish. In Europe sea bass, gilt-head bream and of course salmon are the most common fish being farmed, from Scotland to the Mediterranean. In addition rope-grown mussel farms have made huge inroads in producing large quantities of grit-free mussels. Both rock and native oysters have been farmed for many years. It is certainly acceptable to use farmed salmon instead of their wild-caught cousins as wild salmon

stocks are desperately low. As with most things fish related the decision to choose farmed over wild depends on how the fish look and what has been put into them.

The slightly more worrying side of farming starts to appear when the word 'intensive' is used in the same sentence. Fish are caught using encircling gear mentioned earlier but are then kept in this moving trap while they are fed everything and anything so they build up as much weight as possible. This is particularly common with tuna, where whole shoals are caught and intensively fed. Farming on this commercial scale doesn't really help take demand off stocks.

Finally there are more and more entrepreneurial fish farmers who are taking on other species in an attempt to produce a viable farmed fish. Turbot and halibut are both being successfully farmed in small batches and could be a real help in reducing pressure on these slow-maturing fish.

Fishing for cod

If you love fish – and more importantly, if you care about fish stocks – then at some point you are going to have the 'cod conversation'. Much like tuna, cod is the media darling of the fishing world. Conservationists say stocks are running low and that we should not eat it, while the fishermen say that there is so much of it they can't help but catch it and end up having to throw it back overboard. You will see it on a menu, or at the fish and chip shop and think to yourself 'do I, or don't I?'

The solution to this problem is to make an informed decision. The most important thing a fish lover needs to know about cod is that it is seasonal. It likes cold, choppy waters so goes wherever it can find them. Therefore it's in and around the British inshore waters in the winter, moving to deeper colder waters in the summer. So if you eat cod all year round, then you are not giving the stocks time to recover from being fished. The only way to eat cod with a clear conscience is to make sure it is always fresh and always locally caught. It's also important to know how it was caught. Deep-sea trawlers have no choice in what size they catch (apart from small fish that are able to get through the nets) and although they know where certain fish are they can't guarantee catch. Tidal gill nets are a much more sustainable way of fishing for cod.

It's 5.30am on a blustery morning in the port of Shoreham, East Sussex, when skipper Gary Brownrigg, along with mate Peter Budden, starts up the engine of the Catherine Ann and sets off to check on the nets. He's after cod. There is a small quota for this winter – about ten tonnes, so he only puts his nets out when the price is good. He can charge a premium because of the quality of the fish he catches. He nods at the fish market, as he passes, already a bustle of activity preparing for the arrival of the day's catch.

As he leaves the harbour the swell picks up – nothing to worry about, but his mind returns to when a sudden storm actually flipped the boat over. Fishing is dangerous. There's no point going out when it's really rough, the rocks and stone are thrown around so much they get caught in the nets, ruining them.

Gill nets are a very sustainable way of catching cod. They're placed on the seabed like a tennis court net but the strong current keeps them flat on the bottom until the slack tide, when the nets rise up ready to catch the fish. The tide takes about an hour to turn and the net will then be pushed back onto the seabed. So the nets only fish for a couple of hours a day. They have big holes to let the smaller fish through and although Gary knows where the fish are, they're not stupid – they can see the net and the clever ones simply swim around it.

He pulls and re-sets five nets off the Sussex coast, all inshore where he knows the bigger fish will be and lands a good catch of cod, as well as some ray and Dover sole. He's also caught a few cuttlefish but these will go straight to Spain as there is no market for them in the UK. As noon approaches the last net is set – it's been a good day so he heads back to the safety of the harbour for a mug of tea and a bacon sandwich.

How to buy fish

Of all the foods we buy, fish and shellfish are high on the 'not a clue' chart. With so many types of fish and decisions to make about whether to buy it frozen or fresh, filleted or not, whole or in a tranche, the easiest choice is to let the manufacturer do it for us. Hence our love of the fish finger, fish and chips and the obligatory fish pie. But there are thousands of professional sales people on hand to help: they're called fishmongers.

There is nothing like walking into a fishmongers bursting with some of the best fresh fish and shellfish available. There's the smell of the sea, mixed gently with the aroma of the smoked kippers or fillets and if you are lucky the trickle of water pouring into the tanks full of live crabs or lobsters. Behind this display of the finest produce our island seas have to offer stands your fishmonger, ready to help you make the right choice.

Ask questions

Try to avoid doing this during the Saturday morning rush. A weekday morning is the perfect time to introduce yourself and ask for help. The sort of information a fishmonger needs is how many you want to feed, how easy or complicated you want it to be and how much roughly you want to pay. Then the process of choice can begin. Often the first decision will be between fish and shellfish, then what type, then quantity and price and finally the recipe and whether you want to fillet it at home or have it prepared for you. Fishmongers love talking to customers and offering advice. They are a source of knowledge so take advantage of them!

Buy cookbooks

This is not an obvious plug, as unless you are reading this in a bookshop you've already made this step. Cookbooks can give you plenty of inspiration and the courage to give something a go for the first time. A recipe will tell you what you need to buy and what you need to do so feel free to take the recipe into your fishmongers and ask them for the ingredients. If they don't have it they can often offer an alternative. If you are cooking a fish for the first time have a practice run – rather than risk all for a dinner party, a smaller version can easily be tried and tested, boosting your confidence.

Look at what you are buying

Fish should look fresh, with a clear sheen. Whole fish should have bright eyes and red gills and the flesh should look and feel firm and it should certainly not smell of anything but the sea. Ask if it has been previously frozen. Supermarkets are now demanding more non-frozen fish from their suppliers because freezing fish causes ice crystals to grow between the proteins of the flesh and once defrosted, the fish will start to deteriorate quickly. Buying frozen fish can be a perfectly acceptable option but it's better to defrost it yourself overnight in the fridge. You should also pay less for it.

How to prepare fish

Most fishmongers will skin and fillet your fish for you but if you want to do it yourself, all you need is a sharp filleting knife and a bit of courage. The more you practise, the more skilled you'll become.

Round fish

Many smaller round fish, such as sardines, mackerel or herring, can be cooked whole but they can also be filleted.

Lay the fish on a board with the back away from you and with a sharp filleting knife, lift the gill fin up and cut at an angle behind the fin to remove the head.

Holding the fish firmly, insert the knife flat at the top of the fish and run the blade down the fish feeling the back bone as you go. Pull the flesh away with the other hand as you work. Flip the fish over and repeat the process until both fillets are removed. Keep the bones to make fish stock (see page 33).

Flat fish

Flat fish, such as plaice or sole can be filleted to give four small fillets.

Place the flat fish on a chopping board with the head away from you. Remove the head and cut down the centre or lateral line of the fish down to the back bone. Working on the fillet closest to you, insert the point of the knife under the flesh and start to run the knife down the fillet until the fillet is removed. Turn the fish around and repeat the process until both are removed, then flip the fish over and repeat on the other side to give four fillets.

Shellfish

When cleaning shellfish always discard any with damaged shells as these may give you problems. Similarly throw away any that are gaping open or that do not shut firmly when tapped with the back of a knife. For mussels you need to remove the beard. Holding the mussel in one hand grab hold of the beard with the other and pull it up towards the hinge of the mussel – it should pull out. Rinse mussels and clams under cold water (never leave them covered as they will drown) and scrub them with a brush if they are particularly dirty.

Octopus

Octopus can end up tough and chewy so it's often a good idea to tenderize it before cooking. If you have a whole octopus you need to turn it inside out to remove the guts and beak, as you would for a squid (see page 36). Turn back the right way and then rinse under cold running water before using a rolling pin to hammer away at it before cooking.

Squid (see page 36)

Oysters (see page 46)

Crab (see page 55)

Lobster (see page 145)

25

Starters

Brill fillets with citrus salsa

4 x 150-g brill fillets, skin on
citrus salsa (see page 173),
to serve

Serves 4

Brill is a fantastic-tasting, grossly undervalued flat fish which is abundant around our shores but hardly ever seen in the shops. It produces wonderfully tasty, light fillets, which are very easy to cook and serve. So if you are out to impress with minimal effort, this is the dish to cook.

1 First prepare the citrus salsa and chill in the fridge, ideally for about 20 minutes, but you can use it immediately if you are in a hurry.

2 Preheat the grill to moderate and cover the grill rack with greaseproof paper. Place the brill fillets on top, skin side up and as close to the heat as possible. Grill for 10 minutes or until the skin browns.

3 As soon as the skin starts to bubble remove the rack from the heat and stack the fillets in the centre of four plates. Drizzle with a little citrus salsa and serve.

Sea bass fillets with mango and chilli salsa

4 wild sea bass fillets, cleaned and all small bones removed with tweezers

100 g unsalted butter

olive oil

salt and freshly ground black pepper

mixed salad leaves, to serve

For the mango and chilli salsa

1 ripe mango

2 tablespoons olive oil

1 tablespoon white wine vinegar

1 red chilli

1 tablespoon chopped coriander

1 tablespoon lemon juice

Serves 4

This is an ideal summer dish. Be sure to make the mango salsa by hand, as it will be too smooth if made in a food processor and you will lose all the texture.

1 First make the salsa. Skin the mango, remove the central stone and chop the flesh into very small cubes. Place these in a bowl with the olive oil and vinegar and mix. Cut the chilli in half and remove the seeds to reduce its heat. Take care not to touch your eyes after handling chillies or they will sting. Chop the chilli, add to the mango mixture and stir. Add the chopped coriander and lemon juice and leave to infuse – the flavour of the salsa will improve if it is left in the fridge for a few hours, so it is best to prepare this a little in advance. This is one salsa that does not work if processed in a food processor: the mango will not hold its shape and the mixture will end up looking like a smoothie.

2 Season the sea bass fillets with salt and pepper and turn skin side up. Gently score 3–4 cuts diagonally across the skin. Heat a frying pan until hot, add the butter and a generous slug of olive oil to prevent the butter from burning. Allow the butter to melt then add the fillets skin side down. Cook for 3 minutes until the skin has gone all brown and crispy – check with a spatula. Turn the fillets over skin side up and just cook the flesh for about 30 seconds just to add some colour (the heat would have already cooked the centre of the fillets). Remove from the heat and serve with a generous amount of salsa and some salad leaves.

Note

Wild sea bass get nice and big over the summer as they come close to the shore to feast on mackerel. They are caught by small hook-and-line day boats. This dish looks amazing made with thick fillets so ask your fishmonger to source some hook-and-line fillets for you.

Smoked salmon with horseradish sour cream and rye bread

120 g smoked salmon

120 g hot-smoked salmon

a few mixed salad leaves

4 tablespoons horseradish sour cream (see page 167), to serve

4 lemon wedges

rye bread, in slices, to serve

Serves 4

A simple but effective starter, which is sure to please. The horseradish-flavoured sour cream goes very well with the smoked salmon, adding a pleasant touch of sharpness to the dish. Hot-smoked salmon is cut slightly thicker than the traditional type so combining the two here gives a little bit of variety.

1 First make the horseradish sour cream and chill in the fridge until needed.

2 Divide the salmon between four plates and garnish with the salad leaves. Place the horseradish sour cream in a ramekin or similar small dish on each plate together with the lemon wedges and serve with rye bread.

31

Fishy Fishy fish stew

25 ml olive oil

1 onion, sliced

1 leek, white part only, sliced

1 garlic clove, crushed

1 small fennel bulb, sliced

2 large tomatoes, chopped

small pinch of saffron

1 red chilli, deseeded and chopped

1 teaspoon cayenne pepper

1½ litres fish stock (see note)

500 g mixed fish, cut into bite-sized chunks

1 small bunch parsley

salt and freshly ground black pepper, to taste

crusty bread, to serve

Serves 6

The dish always brings back memories of holidays in France. The secret is to make a good stock, ideally with crab or lobster shells. The first step of the method makes a basic fish soup, which can be a starter or a meal in itself, served with some croûtons, rouille (see page 176) and grated cheese. To make an authentic bouillabaisse stew, however, like those served on the harbourside at Marseille, you will need to add some fish and seafood chunks. This can be any seasonal fish – pink gurnard is a particular favourite as the bones make an excellent stock. Some shell-on prawns or mussels also add great flavour.

1 Heat the olive oil in a saucepan then add the onion, leek, garlic and fennel and sweat until soft, but not brown. Add the tomatoes, saffron, chilli, cayenne pepper, salt and pepper and cook for a further 5 minutes before adding the fish stock. Bring to the boil and simmer for a further few minutes to combine all the flavours. Remove from the heat and allow to cool for 10 minutes. Pour into a blender and process until you have a thick, smooth soup. Pass through a sieve to catch anything you may have missed.

2 Return the soup to a clean pan and bring to a slow boil. Add the fish and seafood mixture. Place a lid on the pot and cook for about 4 minutes, or until the prawns have cooked through and the mussels opened. Spoon into soup dishes, sprinkle some chopped parsley on top and serve with crusty bread.

Fish stock
The success of a good fish soup depends on the stock. Fish stock is really quick to make – after about 20 minutes you're going to get as much flavour out of the shells and fish bones as you need. Melt some butter and add 1 chopped onion. Add 1½ litres water, fish bones, crab, lobster or prawn shells, herbs and seasoning. Add a little white wine if you like. Bring to the boil and simmer for about 20 minutes. The secret of a good fish stock is to crush the shells as much as possible, then carefully sieve the stock before using.

33

Grilled herrings with black pepper and lemon

Herrings are very popular in Scandinavian countries and, grilled simply with black pepper and lemon juice to offset their richness, make a starter that is easy to prepare and elegant to serve.

4 large (400-g) herrings
olive oil
freshly ground black pepper
juice of ½ lemon
a few mixed salad leaves
4 lemon wedges

Serves 4

1 Slice the flesh of the herrings at an angle, rub the olive oil over the skin and season with the black pepper and lemon juice. Place them on a heatproof dish and grill them for about 5 minutes on each side.

2 Remove the herrings from under the grill and serve immediately, with salad leaves and lemon wedges to garnish.

Pickled herrings

600 g herring fillets, skin on

2 tablespoons pickling spices

300 ml white wine vinegar

1 tablespoon lemon juice

125 g granulated sugar

1 large white onion, sliced

Serves 4

Pickled herrings are delicious served on rye bread with a dollop of sour cream but you can also use them to create a salad, with grated cooked beetroot and peppery watercress.

1 Cut the fish fillets into bite-sized pieces, rinse under running cold water then place in a large bowl covered with 250 ml fresh water and 1 tablespoon of the pickling spices. Leave in the fridge for one day. Rinse, then soak again in the white wine vinegar and leave again for a day.

2 To make the pickling liquor, strain the white wine vinegar off the fish and place in a pan along with the remaining pickling spices, the lemon juice, sugar and sliced onions. Bring to a gentle simmer and cook gently until the onions have softened, about 5 minutes. Remove and allow to cool completely.

3 Place the herrings in a sterilized pickling jar and pour in the pickling liquor, making sure the fish is completely covered. Put the lid on and store in the fridge. These will keep for about 5 days once opened, up to 2 weeks if unopened.

35

Squid

Squid is one of the most abundant, sustainable and versatile types of seafood we have in British waters, yet most of it is cleaned, frozen and shipped off to Europe. If you are ever sitting at some lovely beachside restaurant on the Mediterranean coast, enjoying a glass of wine looking across the warm sea eating some *calamari*, the squid is likely to be as British as your sunburn.

Squid is an increasingly popular purchase and is available in a number of different forms. It is caught in every ocean around the globe and is quite possibly the most widely consumed seafood in the world. Fresh squid comes in a variety of sizes – smaller squid are perfect for stir-frying while larger squid can be used for stuffing and braising. It also freezes well. A fresh squid should have pearly white flesh – as it loses condition the flesh starts to turn pink. The membrane on the outside of the squid is delicate and comes away easily when jostled around in a box.

How to prepare squid

• First pull the tentacles away from the main body and then remove the beak from the centre of the tentacles. Inside the middle of the squid is a quill-like cartridge – remove this carefully.

• Now insert a thumb under the wings or fins and pull them away. Pull away the membrane from the body to leave a nice clean squid 'pouch'.

• To open the squid out flat, insert a knife and cut along one side. This large piece can now be cut into smaller rectangles (20 x 5 cm) and scored with diagonal lines.

• For squid rings, simply leave the pouch whole and slice into rings. For a stuffed squid leave whole. The tentacles can be trimmed and sliced into 5-cm lengths and stir-fried.

Chargrilled squid with tomato and chilli jam

2 fresh squid, cleaned and tentacles reserved
1 tablespoon olive oil
1 tablespoon Tomato and chilli jam (see page 174)
freshly ground black pepper

Serves 2

1 Cut along one side of the squid and open out flat to produce a rectangle and then gently score one surface with diagonal lines. Then cut across into 2 or 3 smaller rectangles, depending on the size of the squid pouch. Season with some black pepper.

2 Rub a griddle with olive oil and heat until it is smoking hot. Then add the squid pieces and cook on one side for about 30 seconds, the squid will curl a bit and start to colour. Turn over and cook on the other side for about 20 seconds. Add the tentacles to the pan and cook for about 30 seconds.

3 Serve with a generous dollop of the tomato and chilli jam.

Squid with lemongrass and spring onion

80 g squid, cleaned
1 tablespoon olive oil
1 teaspoon root ginger julienne
1 garlic glove, crushed
1 lemongrass stalk, sliced
1 spring onion, sliced
salt and freshly ground black pepper
juice of 1 lemon
2 tablespoons chopped parsley

Serves 2

1 Cut the squid into flat pieces and then score with diagonal lines (see page 36)

2 Heat the oil in a hot frying pan and then add the squid and shake the pan. Add the ginger, garlic, lemongrass, spring onion, salt and pepper and shake the pan again. When the squid has taken on some colour remove from the heat and add the lemon juice and the parsley and serve.

Teriyaki squid

2 fresh squid
3 tablespoons Teriyaki marinade
juice of 1 lime
1 tablespoon olive oil

Serves 2

1 Prepare the squid (see page 36) and open them out flat. Slice the squid into small rectangles (10 x 5 cm). Use a sharp knife to score diagonal lines across the flesh. Mix together the Teriyaki marinade and lime juice in a non-metallic dish and add the squid pieces. Allow to marinate for about 30 minutes. When you are ready to cook heat a little oil in a frying pan until hot. Add the squid and cook for 30 seconds until the pieces start to curl.

39

Smoked mackerel pâté

This dish enjoyed great popularity in the seventies. It is an excellent dinner party starter which can be served with thin slices of ordinary or Melba toast.

500 g smoked mackerel fillets

50 g horseradish sauce

2 tablespoons double cream

salt and freshly ground black pepper

juice of ½ lemon

1 tablespoon chopped parsley

For the clarified butter

100 g unsalted butter

Serves 4

1 First make the clarified butter. Place the butter in a small pan and heat gently until the butter melts and splits. The solids will float to the surface – carefully skim these off with a flat spoon and discard.

2 Remove the skin from the mackerel fillets and place them in a food processor along with the other ingredients. Whizz together until smooth and creamy and then divide between four ramekins. Top with clarified butter and leave to chill in the fridge until the butter solidifies.

Smoked trout pâté

4 smoked trout fillets

150 ml full-fat cream cheese

1 bunch chives, chopped

juice of ½ lemon

salt and freshly ground black pepper

French bread, to serve

Serves 4

Farmed trout is a totally acceptable option for this dish – do keep your eye out for a local smokehouse.

1 Mash the fillets in a bowl with a fork, add the cream cheese and mix. Add the chives and lemon juice and season to taste. Mix well and spoon into a serving bowl. Serve with French bread.

Smoked salmon pâté

400 g hot-smoked salmon

2 tablespoons horseradish sauce

juice of ½ lemon

200 ml crème fraîche

salt and freshly ground black pepper

French bread, to serve

Serves 4

Wild salmon is probably wasted on a pâté – it's such a premium product that a good organically farmed version is a better alternative. Adjust the amount of horseradish and lemon juice to suit your own taste.

1 Put the hot-smoked salmon, horseradish and lemon juice in a food processor and process until puréed. Pour into a mixing bowl and add the crème fraîche. Mix until smooth then season with salt and pepper and add more lemon juice, to taste.

41

Goat's cheese and caramelized red onion tartlets

1 tablespoon olive oil

3 medium red onions, thinly sliced

6 tablespoons balsamic vinegar

2 sprigs sage, thinly sliced

4 thick slices of chèvre goat's cheese

mixed salad leaves, dressed

salt and freshly ground black pepper

For the shortcrust pastry

100 g unsalted butter, cut into small pieces

200 g plain flour, plus extra for dusting

pinch of salt

1 egg yolk

Makes 4 tartlets, 10 cm in diameter

Goat's cheese and red onion go together very well, as these tartlets demonstrate. This is a good starter to serve to vegetarians, and can also make a light lunch or supper dish.

1 First make the pastry – although if you are pressed for time you can use ready-made pastry. Put the butter, flour and salt in a food processor and process until the mixture resembles fine breadcrumbs. Add the egg yolk and enough cold water to bring the dough to a firm ball. Wrap it in cling film and chill in the fridge for an hour.

2 Roll out the pastry on a floured surface until it is about 5 mm thick. Cut four circles from the pastry and use to line four loose-bottomed fluted tart cases. Cover each pastry circle with baking paper and baking beans and bake blind at 200°C/400°F/gas 6 for about 10 minutes. Remove the baking beans and baking paper and return to the oven for a further 5 minutes. Set aside to cool.

3 Heat the olive oil in a pan and then add the red onion. Cook over a medium heat until the onions start to catch the bottom of the pan. Add the balsamic vinegar and the sliced sage leaves and cook until the mixture starts to caramelize. Season to taste.

4 Spread the mixture between the pastry cases and place the sliced goat's cheese on top. Cook under a preheated grill until golden brown, remove and serve on a bed of dressed salad leaves.

Half pint of prawns with garlic mayonnaise

Serving fresh shell-on prawns in half-pint glasses is an English pub classic. Fresh lemon wedges, garlic mayonnaise and crusty bread is all you need.

500 g large, cooked shell-on prawns

2 tablespoons garlic mayonnaise (see page 169), to serve

2 lemon wedges, to serve

French bread, to serve

Serves 2

1 Arrange the prawns in the glasses (or put them on a plate if you like). Place the garlic mayonnaise in a ramekin or similar small dish on each plate together with the lemon wedges and serve with French bread.

44

Garlic and herb prawns

500 g cooked shell-on
North Atlantic prawns

100 g unsalted butter

1 tablespoon olive oil

2 garlic cloves, crushed

chopped parsley

freshly ground black pepper

French bread, to serve

Serves 2

Prawns are always popular, and garlic seems to enhance their flavour perfectly. You will need finger bowls for this.

1 If your prawns are frozen make sure they are thoroughly defrosted before you start. Pat dry on kitchen paper.

2 Heat a large frying pan until hot and add the butter and olive oil – the oil will stop the butter from burning. Once the butter has melted add the garlic and let it sizzle for about 20 seconds before adding the prawns. These are already cooked so really only need to be warmed through for 1–2 minutes, stirring occasionally.

3 Remove from the heat and serve in a bowl with some black pepper and a scattering of parsley. Serve with some French bread to mop up the juices.

Note
North Atlantic prawns are smaller than those that are flown in from warmer waters but, to my mind, have a far superior taste.

45

Oysters

People either love them or hate them. To some the thought of putting a small wet, salty, slightly mucousy object in your mouth is abhorrent. To others a meal out is incomplete without them.

Oyster myths

I'm afraid scientific tests have shown that there is no direct link to oysters and your libido. The myth has partly come about because oysters have a high zinc content (a half dozen will give you more than 500% of your daily requirement) and zinc is vital for the production of sperm. The downside is alcohol, which not only reduces your libido but also reduces the body's ability to absorb vitamins and minerals from food. So the oysters may help but the glass of wine you're washing down with it won't. However oysters are low in calories: a dozen oysters contain approximately 110 calories and apart from zinc are full of vitamins and minerals like A, B1, B2, C and D, calcium, iodine, iron, potassium, copper, sodium, phosphorous, manganese and sulphur and the all-important omega-3 fatty acids. So oysters won't improve your love life but they will make you healthy.

As with any shellfish, some people have an allergic reaction to oysters but as a whole oysters are clean and safe to eat raw. All oysters have to go through a process called depuration, where clean sea water is passed through the oysters for a couple of days to remove any silt and chemicals. They also have UV light beamed at them which kills any unwanted bacteria. After a couple of days they are clean and ready to ship. Each pack of oysters has its own passport so if there is a bad bunch (often due to storage at the wrong temperature) they can be traced back to source. However if you want to be sure, before you eat an oyster simply touch the outer rim of it with the edge of your fork, if it moves inwards the oyster is alive and good to go. If it doesn't and maybe even smells a bit funny then send them back. Finally avoid spirits when eating them, oysters contain a histamine which can cause problems in weak stomachs with strong spirits.

Types of oysters

There are two main types of oysters available in the UK – native and rock. Rock oysters are the most commonly available as they can be eaten all year round. Native oysters tend to have a season running from September to April. They can be eaten all year round but when the sea warms up in summer they tend to get very milky as they are spawning. Hence natives tend to come at a premium, especially at the start of the season when they are recovering from spawning. The best natives are in late winter when they have had a good feed over the winter months.

Nearly all rock oysters are farmed, often in idyllic parts of the country with clear, clean sea water. Jersey in particular produces vast amounts of rock oysters which travel as far as the Mediterranean. Various sizes can be bought but the British palate prefers size 2 which can easily be swallowed in one gulp.

If you are intending to serve oysters at home you will need to equip yourself with an oyster knife. There are many different types but whatever you do wrap a tea towel thickly around the hand holding the oyster. They can be a bit slippery and tricky to open and, trust me, a trip to casualty can ruin a birthday dinner.

To open put the oyster flat side on top and insert the oyster knife between the layers on the concave side of the shell. It takes a bit of practice but once in you simply need to sever the ligament which holds the top lid down, once this is cut the top shell will come away easily. Then simply pull it back and throw it away. Clean any bits of shell out and cut the ligament under the body of the oyster to release it. Serve on a tray of crushed ice with lemon.

When buying oysters ask how long they have been stored for. While they can last for five days out of water you want them to be as fresh as possible. Ideally pre-order them from your fishmonger to be collected on the day of consumption. Ordering online can often get you next-day delivery directly from the oyster farmer.

Some purists will say the only way to eat oysters is with a squeeze of lemon but these two dressings are a fabulous alternative. Both make enough to dress 12 oysters.

Tomato, lime and coriander dressing

Mix together 2 finely chopped tomatoes, 1 chopped shallot, 2 tbsp lime juice, 4 tbsp olive oil and 1 tbsp chopped coriander. Drizzle over freshly shucked oysters.

Bloody Mary dressing

Mix together 2 tbsp oyster juice, 2 tbsp tomato juice, 1 tbsp vodka, a dash of Tabasco, 1 tsp horseradish sauce and some black pepper (you can tweak the quantities to suit your own taste). Drizzle over freshly shucked oysters and top with some celery cut into julienne strips. Serve with lemon wedges.

Tempura oysters with tomato and chilli jam

4 oysters, shucked and cleaned

flour, for dusting

oil, for deep-frying

tomato and chilli jam
(see page 174), to serve

For the tempura batter

50 g plain flour

50 g cornflour

1 teaspoon baking powder

200 ml ice-cold sparkling water

salt and freshly ground black pepper

Serves 2

This Japanese dish is a must for oyster lovers. The tomato and chilli jam adds a note of heat which goes well with the batter-coated oysters. We like to use the large size 1 oysters but size 2 works just as well.

1 First make the tempura batter. Mix all the dry ingredients in a bowl and add a pinch of salt and some black pepper. Slowly mix in the ice-cold sparkling water (the bubbles make the batter light), a little at a time, until you have a smooth batter. It should slowly come off the back of a tablespoon – if it sticks add more water, if it runs off too quickly it's too thin. Transfer the batter to a container and surround with ice to keep it chilled.

2 Rinse the oyster shells under running cold water (do not use washing-up liquid) and dry. Roll the shucked oysters in some sifted flour.

3 Dip two of the oysters in the batter and carefully place in a deep-fat fryer on its hottest setting. Alternatively, heat the oil in a large wok or pan. It is hot enough when a cube of bread turns golden in 30 seconds. You want the oysters to float, bubbling on the surface, and crisp up. After 20–30 seconds, depending on how hot your oil is, the oysters should be crisp and brown. Remove and place on some kitchen paper while you repeat with the other two oysters.

4 Place the battered oysters back in the shells and serve with the tomato and chilli jam for dipping.

49

Scallops with chorizo

30 g unsalted butter

100 g chorizo, cubed

12 scallops, cleaned

4 spring onions, chopped

juice of ½ lemon

2 tablespoons chopped parsley

crusty bread, to serve

Serves 4

Scallops and chorizo sausage go very well together. Serve this dish with plenty of crusty French bread.

1 Heat the butter in a frying pan until bubbling and add the pieces of chorizo. The oil released by the chorizo will prevent the butter from burning. Once the chorizo starts taking on a dark red colour add the scallops and cook on one side for 1 minute, then turn over and cook for about 30 seconds.

2 Add the white part of the spring onions and cook through for about 10 seconds, just to let the onions take on some heat. Add the lemon juice and parsley, stir for a few seconds and serve with some crusty bread to mop up the juices.

Note

This dish looks great served in the scallop shells. Any good fishmonger will probably give you the shells for free. Give them a wash and place them under the grill or in a hot oven for a few minutes to warm through before placing the scallops in them.

Brown shrimp pâté with garlic croûtes

200 g cooked shell-on brown shrimps

50 g unsalted butter

50 ml double cream

salt and freshly ground black pepper, to taste

For the croûtes

French bread (stale is fine)

garlic salt

Serves 2

Do not attempt this recipe unless you have plenty of willpower: the best way to prepare brown shrimp is to buy them shell-on and then peel by hand. The urge to scoff the lot before attempting the pâté is irresistible.

1 Peel the brown shrimps. Gently melt half the butter in a saucepan. Put the shrimps, melted butter and salt and pepper to taste in a food processor and process for 10 seconds, until they have turned into a paste. Transfer to a bowl and gently add the double cream until you get a pâté-like consistency. If you like it a bit wetter then that's fine, it will make it easier to spread. Pour into two ramekins and set aside.

2 Melt the remaining butter in a pan, skim off the solids and discard. Pour a small amount of the clarified butter on top of each ramekin to seal the pâté in. Allow to cool and chill in the fridge. The pâté will keep for a few days.

3 To make the croûtes cut the French bread into round circles and place on a baking tray. Sprinkle liberally with garlic salt and bake in a warm oven, preheated to 120°C/250°F/gas ½, until hard and brown. Remove and allow to cool.

Note
This recipe also works for potted shrimp: just add a little paprika to the melted butter and make sure the prawns are evenly covered. Don't process the mixture but just put straight into the ramekins, push the prawns down and cover with some of the melted butter to seal.

Scallops with red pepper and coriander salsa

olive oil, for frying

12 scallops, cleaned

juice of ½ lemon

For the salsa

1 x 280-g jar roasted red peppers, drained

1 red onion

2 red chillies, deseeded

juice of 1 lemon

2 tablespoons chopped coriander

50 ml olive oil

Serves 4

The salsa takes only minutes to prepare, and adds freshness and flavour to the scallops.

1 First make the salsa. Roughly chop the peppers, onions and chillies and place in a food processor. Process for about 10 seconds until almost smooth. Add the lemon juice, chopped coriander and a generous slug of olive oil. Process for a further 10 seconds until the mixture looks like a red paste. Add a little more olive oil if you want it to be smoother. Remove and put into a small bowl. Garnish the salsa with a little more coriander if you wish.

2 Add some olive oil to a hot frying pan and heat until it starts to smoke. Add the scallops and cook on one side for 30 seconds. The oil will spit, so be careful. Turn over and cook for another 30 seconds until the scallops have a nice brown tinge to them. Add a little lemon juice and transfer to warmed plates. Drizzle the scallops with the salsa, sprinkle over a little more coriander and serve.

Note

This is the easy version. You can roast the peppers yourself and make the salsa chunkier by chopping the vegetables into bite-sized pieces and not processing.

53

Clam Chowder

300 g live clams, washed

25 g butter

3 garlic cloves, crushed

50 g smoked pork belly, cut into 1-cm cubes

1 onion, chopped

1 carrot, chopped

1 tablespoon plain flour

3 white potatoes, chopped

1 bay leaf

300 ml fish stock

100 ml single cream

1 tablespoon chopped fresh parsley

freshly ground black pepper

Serves 2

Clam chowder is pretty much an American institution: at every presidential inauguration since 1981 the same clam chowder has been served from the same restaurant in Boston. However, Britain has an abundance of fresh clams around the coast, so make use of them by trying this fabulous comfort food dish.

1 Fill a saucepan with 1 cm water and place a steamer tray inside. Cover and bring to the boil and then tip in the clams. Steam for 5 minutes, or until they are all open. Drain the clams in a colander, taking care to reserve the clam juice. Tip this into a sieve lined with kitchen paper to remove any grit and set aside. Remove the clams from their shells then chop them and rinse under running cold water.

2 Melt the butter in the bottom of a good saucepan. Add the garlic to the melted butter and cook gently for 1 minute. Add the pork belly to the saucepan, fry briefly then add the onion and carrot and cook for 1–2 minutes, just until they get a little colour. Add the flour and mix in to soak up all the juice. Add the potatoes, the clam juice, bay leaf and the fish stock until all the vegetables are covered. Simmer gently for 10 minutes, until they are tender.

3 Add the clams and cook gently for a further 5 minutes – the clams are already cooked so you just want to warm them through or they will turn too rubbery. Remove the chowder from the heat and set aside.

4 When you are ready to serve, remove the bay leaf and reheat the chowder without bringing it to the boil. Slowly trickle in the cream, stirring it in as you go. Remove from the heat and serve in deep bowls with freshly ground black pepper and some chopped parsley.

Note
The juice from steamed clams should never be wasted, as it makes a perfect seafood stock for a host of dishes. Surprisingly, the addition of smoked pork belly really complements the flavour of the clams, rather than dominating it.

Devilled crab

1 x 500-g medium crab, cooked
50 g unsalted butter
1 teaspoon cayenne pepper
juice of ½ lemon
1 tablespoon chopped chives
granary rolls, to serve
lemon wedges, to serve

Serves 4

Devilled dishes were very popular in the 19th century. Meat, fish and egg dishes are flavoured with piquant spices. Crab lends itself very well to devilling.

1 Stand the cooked crab on its head, pushing against its underside with your thumbs and lever away the back end of the shell. Remove and discard the grey-white stomach sac which is behind the head in the shell. Remove and discard the grey feathered gills (also known as the dead mens' fingers), which lie on either side of the body. Pick out the crab meat in the shell using a crab pick or similar instrument and place the claws on a chopping board. Crack the claws and extract the meat from them.

2 Once you have got as much meat as you can out of the crab place it all in a bowl and gently mix it together with your hands. You are both breaking the larger chunks up and also checking for small bits of the skeleton which may have been picked as well. Once you are happy with the mixture you should have enough meat for about four servings.

3 Melt the butter in a saucepan and add the cayenne pepper. Add the crab mixture and stir through (if the crab was very large, you may not be able to use all the meat). The crab meat should have a glossy, red tinge to it. Mix in the lemon juice. As the crab meat is already cooked you just want to warm it through so it will only need 1 minute. Remove from the heat, mix in some chopped chives and divide between four ramekins. Alternatively, press the mixture into four ring moulds. Leave to chill in the fridge.

4 To serve, place a ramekin on the centre of the plate or push the crab mixture out of the mould. Serve with warm granary rolls and lemon wedges.

Note
When buying crabs: if you like white meat go for the cocks (males), which have bigger claws that yield more white meat, but if you prefer brown meat then choose the hens (females), which have more meat in their heads.

55

Trio of eggs

Sometimes you just want something different for breakfast. These three dishes are easy to make and provide a great start to the day. We love using crumpets as they make a good base and hold their shape well. Thickly sliced toast or traditional English muffins also work well.

Eggs Royale

1 slice hot-smoked salmon (this is thicker than normal smoked salmon)

1 crumpet, toasted

1 egg, poached

Hollandaise sauce

freshly ground black pepper

Serves 1

1 Put the smoked salmon slice on the crumpet, top with the poached egg and pour Hollandaise sauce over. Season with black pepper and serve.

Eggs Florentine

1 handful baby spinach, microwaved on high for 20 seconds until wilted

1 crumpet, toasted

1 egg, poached

Hollandaise sauce

freshly ground black pepper

Serves 1

1 Put the wilted spinach on the crumpet, top with the poached egg and pour Hollandaise sauce over. Season with black pepper and serve.

Eggs Benedict

1 slice unsmoked free-range ham

1 crumpet, toasted

1 egg, poached

Hollandaise sauce

freshly ground black pepper

Serves 1

1 Put the ham slice on a crumpet, top with the poached egg and pour Hollandaise sauce over. Season with black pepper and serve.

Deep-fried calamari with lemon crème fraîche

plain flour, for dusting

600 g squid rings

300 ml semi-skimmed milk

oil, for deep-frying

salt and freshly ground black pepper

lemon crème fraîche
(see page 167), to serve

Serves 4

Deep-fried squid rings (calamari) make a delicious, easy starter. The lemon crème fraîche is a perfect foil for them. Serve with a few mixed salad leaves for an attractive presentation.

1 First make the lemon crème fraîche and chill in the fridge until needed.

2 Sprinkle some plain flour in a dish and season it. Place the squid rings in the flour and shake, making sure they are well covered. Dip them in milk and then in flour again. Shake off any excess flour. Place in the deep-fryer and fry until crisp, shaking the basket so the squid rings do not stick together. Alternatively, cook in batches in a large pan or wok, again making sure that the rings do not stick together. Remove and drain on kitchen paper to absorb any excess oil. Serve hot with lemon crème fraîche.

59

Barbecue

& al fresco eating

Albacore tuna salad

4 large albacore tuna steaks

olive oil, for rubbing

salt and freshly ground black pepper

For the salad

250 g mixed salad leaves

125 g new potatoes, cooked, cooled and chopped

125 g green beans, blanched

125 g cherry tomatoes, halved

1 red onion, cut into slices

50 g pitted black olives

salad dressing (see page 175)

Serves 4

Albacore tuna follows the shoals of squid and smaller fish from the Mediterranean up to the waters of Cornwall. It is the only guilt-free tuna available to the local British market, although there are improvements to methods being used in the southern Indian Ocean. It has a great taste, is very meaty in texture and can be used in a variety of ways, which is why it is dubbed the chicken of the sea.

1 First make the salad. Place the salad leaves in a large mixing bowl and add the new potatoes, green beans, tomatoes, sliced red onion and black olives. Drizzle over some salad dressing, mix well and place in four bowls.

2 Rub the tuna steaks with the oil and season. Heat a griddle pan until smoking hot and add the tuna steaks. Sear for about 3 minutes, turning halfway through to give you griddle lines on the steak.

3 Place the tuna steaks on top of the salad and serve.

Mixed seafood kebabs

600 g mixed white fish, such as pollock or huss

4 tablespoons olive oil, plus extra for grilling

16 scallops

4 red peppers, deseeded and cut into large dice

2 red onions, cut into large dice

salt and freshly ground black pepper

Makes 8 skewers

These kebabs are great for summer barbecues and make an interesting change from the usual burgers and sausages.

1 Soak eight wooden skewers in water for about 30 minutes to stop them burning when you cook the kebabs. Cut the fish into chunks and place in a large bowl, along with the scallops. Drizzle the olive oil over the fish and season.

2 Thread each skewer alternately with the fish, scallops, peppers and onions until all the ingredients are used up. Place the kebabs on a tray and drizzle the oil left in the bowl over them and chill until you are ready to cook.

3 Rub a little oil on to the barbecue grill and lay the skewers on top. Allow 3–5 minutes each side so the heat can penetrate through the flesh before turning. Each side will need slightly less time than the one before. After 3 or 4 turns remove the kebabs. Either serve them on the skewers or push all the barbecued ingredients into a big bowl for sharing.

Brown trout with lemon and dill butter

125 g unsalted butter, diced
juice of 1 lemon
½ bunch dill
4 x 400–500-g brown trout
freshly ground black pepper
new potatoes, to serve

Serves 4

Trout is such a delicious fish that it doesn't require over-fussy presentation. Dill, with its aniseed flavour, is a perfect foil for the earthy fish.

1 Make the lemon and dill butter. Place the butter and some black pepper into a food processor and start to process. Slowly add the lemon juice then, when the mixture is stiff, add the dill and process for just a few seconds so it doesn't break up too much. Remove the butter from the processor and place on a sheet of greaseproof paper. Roll it into a sausage shape and chill in the fridge until needed.

2 Fill the cavity of each fish with some of the dill and lemon butter and place on a baking tray with a couple more pats of the flavoured butter on top. Bake in the oven, preheated to 200°C/400°F/gas 6, for 8–10 minutes, until the flesh is slightly firm to the touch. Remove the trout from the oven and add another slice of lemon and dill butter on top of each. Serve with new potatoes.

65

Marinated Asian-style fish fillets

8 x 150-g black bream or sea bass fillets

50 ml soy sauce

25 g brown sugar

1 large red chilli, deseeded and chopped

3 garlic cloves, crushed

1 x 5-cm piece root ginger, peeled and chopped

6 spring onions, sliced

1 tablespoon sesame seeds

1 bunch coriander, chopped

butter and oil, for frying

mixed salad leaves, to serve

Serves 4

Barbecued food calls for robust flavours and this Asian-inspired marinade lends itself well to the fish fillets, tenderizing the flesh at the same time.

1 Score the skin of the fish fillets, taking care not to go all the way through to the flesh.

2 Put the soy sauce, sugar, chopped chilli, garlic, ginger, spring onions, sesame seeds and coriander in a large non-metallic bowl and whisk together to make the marinade. Place the fish fillets in the mixture and allow to marinate for 1–2 hours.

3 Put a heavy frying pan or griddle pan over a medium heat and add a knob of butter and a little olive oil. Remove the fillets from the marinade, shaking off any excess and fry the fish, skin side down, for about 8 minutes, until golden brown. Turn over and let the heat in the pan finish the fillets off. Serve with mixed salad leaves.

Crab and lobster Niçoise salad

4 large handfuls mixed salad leaves

150 g cooked new potatoes, quartered

40 g cherry tomatoes

40 g black olives, pitted

150 g cooked fine green beans

salad dressing (see page 175)

150 g white crab meat

150 g lobster meat

4 poached eggs (see note below)

Serves 4

A more elegant and upmarket version of the standard Niçoise salad, which is ideal for entertaining.

1 Line a large dish with the salad leaves. Place the quartered new potatoes, cherry tomatoes, black olives and green beans in a bowl and drizzle over some salad dressing. Mix gently by hand until evenly covered and then arrange over the salad leaves in the dish.

2 Break up the crab and lobster meat with a fork and place over the salad. Poach the eggs (see note) and place on top of the salad to finish.

Note
The perfect way to poach an egg is to bring a saucepan to the boil, then, once it is bubbling, swirl around a spoon to make a small whirlpool. Break an egg into the middle and remove the pan from the heat. Leave for 1–2 minutes then take the poached egg out of the pan. Drain on kitchen paper while you cook the other eggs.

68

A smoking hot mackerel salad

250 g new potatoes

8 marinated artichokes, sliced in half

80 g radishes, sliced

80 g spring onions, sliced

80 g cooked beetroot, sliced

salad dressing (see page 175)

4 handfuls mixed salad leaves

8 hot-smoked mackerel fillets

Serves 4

This is a gutsy, very flavoursome salad, which is ideal to serve at a summer party and very quick to make.

1 Boil the potatoes until tender, drain and rinse under cold water to stop the cooking process. Once cold slice or quarter.

2 Put the potatoes, artichokes, radishes, spring onions and beetroot in a large bowl. Drizzle with the salad dressing and toss gently with your hands. Divide the leaves between four plates and top with the dressed salad. Finish each plate with two mackerel fillets.

3 Spoon over a little more of the dressing and serve immediately.

Note
Fish can be hot- or cold-smoked. Hot-smoking means the fish is put directly over the fire, a method which is often used for mackerel. Cold-smoking is where the smoke is diverted off the fire, cooled and then allowed to flavour the fish – a method often used with smoked salmon.

69

Sea bass with summer herbs and lime

2 x 500–600-g whole wild line-caught sea bass, skin on, gutted and scaled

1 tablespoon sunflower oil

salt and freshly ground black pepper

For the marinade

a large handful of fresh herbs, such as marjoram, parsley, basil, dill or oregano

1 lime

2 tablespoons pomace olive oil

Serves 2

Wild sea bass, preferably line-caught, is a great fish to put on the barbecue. Its thicker skin keeps the high heat at bay while sealing in the firm white flesh. Sea bass does not need its great taste to be hidden but supported with a selection of the freshest herbs.

1 First make the marinade. Finely chop all the herbs, top and tail the lime and dice, skin and all. Mix together in a separate bowl with the olive oil and set aside.

2 Carefully remove all the fins from the sea bass, taking care as the dorsal fins are quite sharp. Leave the head on and gently score both sides of the fish. Rub the marinade into the skin and into the cavity of the fish. Season with salt and pepper and chill in the fridge for 20 minutes.

3 Preheat the barbecue and rub the grill with sunflower oil. Alternatively, put the sea bass in a fish holder and place on the hot grill. Cook for about 6 to 8 minutes on each side, until the inner flesh starts to turn white.

4 Serve whole with new potatoes.

Notes

If you can't get sea bass, a red mullet or any thick-skinned fish will do. Red mullet is a smaller fish and you should reduce the cooking time accordingly.

Pomace olive oil is obtained from the second pressing of the olives and has a higher smoking point than other oils.

71

Cracked lobster and crab claws

Most good fishmongers will have a good supply of crab claws on display, a by-product of boiling off the catch. They will be unlikely to sell lobster claws on their own so you will have to invest in a whole lobster. You can always cut up and freeze the main body for a luxury lobster linguine treat (see page 150) or even a lobster salad. One 600–800-g lobster will serve 1, and a 900-g will serve 2.

1 Cook the whole lobster for about 5 minutes per kg and then set aside. Remove the claws by hand and place in a bowl of cold water to cool. The crab claws should already be cooked but if not, put them into the boiling water used for the lobster and heat through for 5 minutes, then add them to the cooling lobster claws. Once cooled crack each part of the claw using a large chef's knife or set of crab crackers. Split the claws and serve with Marie Rose sauce (see page 166) and garlic mayonnaise (see page 169).

Grilled triggerfish with salsa verde

4 triggerfish fillets

pomace olive oil (see note, page 71) or ordinary olive oil

salt and freshly ground black pepper

salsa verde (see page 173), to serve

Serves 2

Triggerfish is a funny little character. It looks a bit like bream with a tall oval-shaped body which is perfect for nestling into cracks between rocks to hide from predators. They like warmer waters so you won't find them in winter. However, their large sides produce delicious white fillets.

1 Line a baking sheet with greaseproof paper and drizzle with oil, then sprinkle on some salt and pepper. Place the triggerfish fillets on the baking sheet.

2 Preheat the grill to high. Place the fillets under the grill and cook for about 8 to 10 minutes. Serve with salsa verde.

Barbecued herrings with citrus butter

4 x 400-g herrings, cleaned but with head and tail still on

olive oil

100 g citrus butter (see page 170)

salt and freshly ground black pepper

Serves 4

Herrings, simply cooked and served with citrus butter, make a popular barbecue dish.

1 Rub each herring with olive oil and season with salt and pepper. Rub some more oil on to the grill tray to prevent the fish from sticking and cook on a hot barbecue for 6–8 minutes each side. Once you have turned the herrings on to the second side, add a knob of citrus butter on top of each herring to melt.

73

Barbecued mackerel with Jonathon's Uruguayan potato salad

600 g new season's Jersey potatoes

4 spring onions

4 tablespoons mayonnaise (see page 169)

pinch of cayenne pepper

4 medium mackerel, cleaned and gutted

olive oil

salt and freshly ground black pepper

tomato and onion salad, to serve

Serves 4

Mackerel is a seasonal summer fish which comes inshore during the summer from May to about October. It is an easy fish to catch and a morning fishing trip for an hour should produce sufficient amounts for a good summer afternoon barbecue.

Potato salad, much like the British summer, can often be a disappointment. There is so much anticipation only to be let down by a dull and wet offering. This recipe, introduced to be by my friend Jonathon, who has been making it for over 20 years, came from his Uruguayan mother.

1 Fill a saucepan with salted water and bring to the boil. Add the potatoes and cook until tender (about 10 minutes). Plunge into cold water to stop the cooking process and allow to cool for 20 minutes. Halve or quarter.

2 Finely chop the spring onions and mix with the mayonnaise and a pinch of cayenne pepper. Mix into the new potatoes and season to taste. Be warned, the heat from the cayenne takes some time to develop. This will refrigerate for a couple of days but is best eaten on the same day.

3 Score the flesh of the mackerel at an angle and rub each fish with olive oil and salt and pepper. Place the mackerel on the barbecue and cook for 5–6 minutes each side. When cooked, transfer the fish to four serving plates and serve with a good heap of potato salad and a tomato and onion salad.

74

Prawn cocktail

600 g cooked shell-on prawns, thawed if frozen

4 tablespoons Marie Rose sauce (see page 166)

½ iceberg lettuce

8 lemon wedges, to serve

pinch of cayenne pepper

dash of Tabasco (optional)

Serves 4

Something of a seventies retro classic, the prawn cocktail survives in many forms to this day. From mechanically peeled, tasteless pink blobs, to large wild-caught jumbo prawns, it is found all over the world. For a constant supply of sustainable shell-on prawns, the North Atlantic delivers the best source and this is one time you want them cooked and frozen on board ship. However, if you live by a sandy beach, ideally with a long tide, then it should easily be possible to source some local prawns.

1 Peel the prawns, trying not too eat too many of them, but reserve at least 12 for a garnish.

2 Mix the peeled prawns gently into the sauce. Shred the iceberg lettuce and fill about a third of four large wine glasses with it. Then add a good dollop of the prawn cocktail mixture on top. Finally, garnish with the reserved prawns (hanging 3 over the rim of each glass) and a couple of lemon wedges per serving. Sprinkle some cayenne pepper over the top and add a dash of Tabasco, if liked, for an extra kick.

Note
The perfect prawn cocktail delivers in just one spoonful a hint of spice from the Tabasco, a cool dollop of the prawn coated in the thick sauce and then a bit of crunch from the lettuce. A timeless classic.

BBQ oysters

12 rock oysters

For the barbecue sauce

5 tablespoons tomato ketchup

1 tablespoon brown sugar

pinch of cayenne pepper

pinch of smoked paprika

½ shallot, very finely chopped

1 garlic clove, crushed

pinch of allspice

pinch of ground cinnamon

pinch of ground mace

pinch of black pepper

Serves 2

This is a pretty unconventional way of cooking oysters – we discovered that if you put scrubbed unshucked oysters on a barbecue they will just pop open when cooked.

1 First make the barbecue sauce. Place all ingredients in a saucepan and heat over a low heat until the sugar has dissolved. Allow to cool and store in an airtight container until needed.

2 If you don't want to barbecue the oysters, shuck them and arrange them in their shells on a baking tray. Drizzle a teaspoon of the barbecue sauce over each one and cook under a hot grill for 2–3 minutes. Alternatively, put them straight on to the barbecue until they steam or pop open. Remove with tongs (the shells will be very hot), then add the sauce to them.

A family dinner

Customers often ask where the name Fishy Fishy came from. There was no in-depth brand identity development and we didn't ask a thousand people what they thought of the name. It is simply what we always used to say to each other when we were thinking about cooking and eating some fish. Typically one of us would say 'how about everyone coming over to ours tonight for some Fishy Fishy?'

For years we've all fished out of Brighton or nearby Newhaven harbour. If we can, we try and go out together or simply catch a ride on a friend's boat. After a day or even an afternoon out on the water, we usually have a decent selection of fresh local fish to arrange an impromptu get-together. Back home the fish are dumped in the kitchen sink while someone grabs a few cold beers from the fridge.

It became a rule that anyone not on the boat doesn't have to take part in preparing the fish so it's left to one of us to gut, clean and fillet the day's catch. Whether it's a 2-kg pollock or 25 mackerel, it needs to be ready for the pan, oven or barbecue. Then, talk turns to what goes best with what, whether to marinate or to leave untouched and allow the fresh sea taste to permeate. One hard and fast rule is that nothing is fussed over. Any accompaniment must enhance but not dominate the fantastic taste of the fish – and we try to stick to this rule in the restaurant too.

After an hour or so the beer has been replaced with a cold glass of white wine and the table is set, inside or out depending on the weather. The food is served often in the dish it was cooked in, with some seasonal vegetables or a salad. Then the serious talking starts...

It was round the dinner table that we first started talking about the idea for the restaurant and whether people wanted fresh, local and seasonal fish and shellfish. It was round the dinner table when Dermot said he wanted to get involved (well actually it was his partner, Dee). And it is round the dinner table that we still talk about fish, kids, food, TV projects (Dee is a successful director), Posh Totty Designs (my wife's jewellery business) and of course whatever project Dermot is working on. We are not a family in the literal sense, but Fishy Fishy has come to feel like a family to us – it ties us together and gives us plenty to talk about.

We eat, we drink and we laugh and Oliver, if you are reading this when you are older and wondering why you're not in any of the pictures, it's because you were two and in bed. Sorry!

Hot and spicy prawns

600 g cooked shell-on prawns, thawed if frozen

large knob of butter

2 tablespoons chopped coriander

For the spicy paste

30 g smoked paprika

30 g ground cumin

30 g ground coriander

10 g cayenne pepper

120 ml olive oil

40 g brown sugar

salt and freshly ground black pepper

Serves 4

These spicy prawns are guaranteed to wake up your taste buds. Serve with plenty of crusty bread for mopping up the buttery juices.

1 First make the spicy paste. Place all the ingredients in a mixing bowl and stir well to combine. This will keep for a couple of weeks in an airtight container.

2 Place about a tablespoon of the spicy paste in a large frying pan and heat over a medium heat. Add the prawns and shake the pan to cover the prawns in the paste. When the prawns are warmed through add the butter and a splash of warm water to make a sauce. Sprinkle over some fresh coriander and serve with finger bowls (this dish is very messy).

Cornish sardines with pesto

12 fresh Cornish sardines
(pilchards)

olive oil, for drizzling

salt and freshly ground black
pepper

For the pesto

2 handfuls fresh basil leaves

40 g pine nuts

40 g grated Parmesan

1 garlic clove, crushed

150 ml olive oil

salt and freshly ground black
pepper

Serves 4

Cornish sardines are actually pilchards, which are readily
available from most fishmongers right through summer.
You could also use herrings for this recipe.

1 Make the pesto. Place the basil leaves, pine nuts, Parmesan, garlic,
salt and pepper in a food processor and purée until smooth. With the
motor running, drizzle in the olive oil until the pesto has a consistency
you are happy with. This will keep in the fridge for 1–2 days.

2 Drizzle some olive oil over the sardines and season with salt and
pepper. Place them carefully on a hot barbecue and cook for a few
minutes, or until they have turned golden brown. Try to avoid moving
the fish too much as they may break apart. Flip the sardines over and
allow to cook over the heat for another minute or two. When the fins
are getting charred remove and place on a serving dish. Drizzle a
spoonful of pesto over each fish and serve.

82

Chargrilled gurnard with saffron mayonnaise and samphire

2 x 600-g gurnard, filleted

oil, for cooking

salt and freshly ground black pepper

175 g samphire

25 g unsalted butter, melted

For the saffron mayonnaise

4 tablespoons mayonnaise (see page 169)

pinch of saffron

Serves 2

There are two main types of gurnard, grey and pink, found in British waters. The grey gurnard tends to be a larger fish and is available early in the spring, whereas the smaller pink gurnard is available in high summer. Both feed mainly on prawns and crabs on the seabed so have a fantastic flavour to them. Samphire is a seasonal crop, at its best in the high summer months. It's often called the asparagus of the sea because the season is so short and it's used much the same way asparagus is.

1 Make the saffron mayonnaise. Stir a pinch of saffron into the mayonnaise and set aside.

2 Oil and season the fish fillets and place skin side down over a barbecue or skin side up if you are cooking under a grill. After 5 minutes, and once the skins look crispy, turn over and cook for a further 1–2 minutes.

3 Meanwhile cook the samphire in a large pan of boiling water or in a steamer for 1–2 minutes until just tender. Drain and toss in the melted butter. Season with black pepper and serve with the grilled fish and saffron mayonnaise.

Warm mackerel salad with rhubarb chutney

The slightly tart flavour of the rhubarb cuts through the oily and meaty flavour of the mackerel perfectly.

10–12 new potatoes

4 handfuls salad leaves

1 red onion, finely sliced

4 tomatoes, sliced

salad dressing (see page 175)

4 smoked mackerel fillets

For the rhubarb chutney

500 g fresh rhubarb

100 g soft brown sugar

1 cinnamon stick

3 tablespoons red wine vinegar

Serves 4

1 First make the chutney. Slice the rhubarb into 2-cm pieces and place in a saucepan. Add the brown sugar, the cinnamon stick and red wine vinegar and stir until the mixture has reduced and starts to thicken. Remove from the heat and allow to cool. Place in a plastic container. This will keep in the fridge for up to a week.

2 Cook the new potatoes in a large pan of boiling salted water, about 10–15 minutes. Drain and leave to cool and then halve or quarter, depending on the size.

3 Divide the salad leaves between four plates. Mix the red onion, tomatoes and new potatoes together then place them over the leaves and drizzle over the dressing.

4 Grill the mackerel fillets for a few minutes on one side only then remove the skin. Top each plate of salad with flakes of the warm smoked mackerel and serve with the rhubarb chutney.

Note
Mackerel is a great source of natural Omega 3 oils, and is a healthy food choice. So a mackerel a day could literally keep the doctor away.

Barbecued bream with spring onion, coriander and ginger

4 x 450–500-g wild black bream, cleaned and gutted

1 bunch fresh coriander, chopped

6 spring onions, finely sliced

1 x 5-cm piece root ginger, peeled and finely chopped

20 ml light soy sauce

salt and freshly ground black pepper

Serves 4

There is a lot of farmed bream on the market these days, mainly from the Mediterranean, so make sure you ask for wild bream. They usually appear in British waters in early summer and last until July. Farmed bream is an acceptable alternative but make sure you are not paying a premium price for an inferior product.

1 Place the bream on a chopping board and, with a sharp knife, score the skin diagonally at intervals, not all the way through but deep enough to rub the marinade in.

2 Put the chopped coriander, spring onions and root ginger in a bowl. Season with salt and pepper then add the light soy sauce to make a paste. Rub this all over the bream and into the cuts.

3 Place the bream in a fish holder, close it and place on the barbecue. After about 5 minutes turn over and repeat. Place the tip of a small sharp knife in one of the cuts on the fish near the back bone and pull the flesh apart so you can see the back bone. When the flesh has turned white all the way through the fish is cooked. Remove and serve.

Homemade taramasalata and humous

These classic Greek dips are great served with pitta or other flatbreads or grissini – or as an accompaniment.

Taramasalata

1 slice white bread, crusts removed

2 tablespoons milk

250 g smoked cod roe

3 egg yolks

1 onion, shredded

1 tablespoon garlic purée

juice of 1 lemon

200 ml olive oil

salt and freshly ground black pepper

Serves 4

1 Soak the bread in the milk for 10 minutes. Strain off the milk and place the bread in a food processor with all other ingredients except the olive oil. Blend until smooth. With the motor running, slowly add the oil until well combined. Season to taste and serve with warmed pitta bread.

Humous

1 x 400-g tin chickpeas, drained and rinsed

50 g tahini (see note below)

1 tablespoon garlic purée

juice of 2 lemons

salt and freshly ground black pepper

Serves 4

1 Place the chickpeas in a food processor and pulse until broken down slightly then add all the other ingredients and purée until smooth. Season to taste. Serve in ramekins with warmed pitta bread. For a more colourful version mix in some ready-prepared smoked red peppers to make roasted pepper humous.

Note
Tahini is a paste made from sesame seeds, found in any good supermarket or delicatessen.

Everyday fish
& shellfish

Classic fishburgers

600 g line-caught pollock fillet
(or any other white fish),
skinned and boned

1 large shallot, peeled and sliced

1 tablespoon cornichons

1 tablespoon capers

2 tablespoons chopped parsley

flour, for dusting

2 tablespoons olive oil

salt and freshly ground black
pepper

6 ciabatta rolls, to serve

1 large tomato, sliced

few lettuce leaves

mayonnaise

Makes 6

Homemade fishburgers are infinitely superior to the shop-bought variety and are very quick and easy to make.

1 Dice the fish into 5-cm cubes, place in a food processor and process to a rough purée. Transfer the purée to a large mixing bowl. Put the shallot, cornichons, capers, parsley and seasoning in the food processor and purée until evenly blended. Tip out and mix with the fish purée.

2 With floured hands, shape the mixture into 6 burgers. Chill in the fridge for 1 hour to firm up.

3 Heat the olive oil in a frying pan over medium heat and fry the fishburgers, two at a time. Cook for about 5 minutes on each side, or until nicely browned. Take care not to overheat the pan or the fishburgers will burn. Once cooked through and crispy set aside and cook the remaining burgers. Serve in a ciabatta roll with a slice of tomato, a lettuce leaf and some mayonnaise.

Mackerel fishing

What is a perfect day, a day you look forward to and think about long afterwards? It could be a wedding, Christmas or simply a family Sunday lunch. Here at Fishy Fishy it's a day spent fishing for mackerel.

Mackerel has been around UK shores for thousands of years. They were caught by the Romans and have been celebrated by many famous authors, from Charles Dickens and Samuel Pepys through to the food writers of today. With their silver bellies and green and blue tiger stripes their beauty is only surpassed by the flavour of their meat, full of Omega 3 and vitamin B12. There are also millions of them around our shores.

They like our calmer warmer waters so can be found from May to November feeding on squid and anything else smaller than them. They travel in shoals close to the surface and can be found inshore and around river openings and marinas as well as further out to sea. All this makes them easier to catch; you don't have to travel very far from land to fish for them and when you hit a shoal you're going to get more than one.

Usually we hit the boat around 10am, rod and feathers in hand (a feather is a series of six hooks with a little feather attached, which is all you need to attract them). As the boat heads out to sea we sit and catch up. Conversations can vary from the week's menu specials, ideas for new recipes or who is going to catch the most/biggest/first fish. Often a few friends come along, some new, some old hands. Mackerel like a nice clear, sunny day so it can be quite a relaxing sociable time.

After about half an hour the boat engines slow and preparations start for the big hunt. There are plenty of rods available for all but there are always a few more competitive ones who will bring their own and secretly attach their latest hook and feather combination. As the engine stops the skipper has a quick look at the fish finder and announces it's okay to drop the lines. Each rod has a small weight attached to send the sparkly hooks quickly down to the desired depth, around 10 metres. If you've hit a shoal you'll probably get a hit pretty quickly but sometimes you have to wait for them to fall for the brightly coloured flashes of sunlight under the water, looking to them like a small fish, or maybe a squid.

Mackerel fishing is very democratic: no-one knows who is going to get the first bite. But when they do you will all be pulling them in as fast as you can. Rod-and-line-caught mackerel is a totally sustainable way of catching the fish so as soon as one is caught the race is on to get the feathers back in the water as fast as possible before the shoal moves on. Once the first fish is caught and the person responsible is suitably rewarded with a nod of respect, the race is on to catch the biggest and the most fish. In the interests

of sustainability a mental log is kept of how many are caught and any small ones are simply returned to the sea to be caught another day.

Once the shoal has moved away, the skipper will tell us to pull in the lines and head off to another promising spot. This is the time to try a bit of fresh sashimi. You'd be amazed how good a freshly sliced fillet tastes with a bit of soy sauce and wasabi.

After a few more stops enough fish is caught to satisfy our greedy appetites and the boat turns back towards the harbour. The beers are broken out and the fish are sorted into keepers and those thrown back into the sea. Then the arguments start over the fish count... 'No, you can't count the one that escaped from the hook just before you could get hold of it', 'No, being out of the water does not mean it was caught'.

The keepers are quickly dispatched with a chop to the back of the head and then cleaned, gutted and distributed equally. The seagulls follow the boat into shore, screaming at the chance of any easy lunch.

As the boat moors up, the crew are tipped and the happy band place their wobbly legs back on dry land. A plan emerges for the barbecue later that evening, where the debate over the biggest catch will continue well into the night.

Sticky mackerel

4 x 500–600-g mackerel, cleaned and gutted

olive oil, for frying

salt and freshly ground black pepper

For the sticky sauce

50 ml ketchup

25 g brown sugar

¼ teaspoon cayenne pepper

½ teaspoon smoked paprika

1 teaspoon onion powder

1 teaspoon crushed garlic

½ teaspoon allspice

½ teaspoon ground cinnamon

½ teaspoon mace

½ teaspoon ground black pepper

Serves 4

Mackerel, being an oily fish, are a healthy option. Try this recipe for whole mackerel with a sticky sauce for a burst of flavour.

1 First make the sticky sauce. Place all ingredients in a non-reactive saucepan and bring slowly to the boil. Simmer for 5 minutes then allow to cool. Set aside until needed.

2 Preheat the oven to 180°C/350°F/gas 4. Make small cuts along both sides of the mackerel and season inside and outside the fish. Heat some olive oil in a frying pan until smoking then char each side of the fish for a few minutes. Transfer the mackerel to a roasting dish and put in the preheated oven.

3 After about 10 minutes take out the fish and paint the sticky sauce across the top of the fish. Return to the oven for a further 5 minutes until the sauce looks thick and sticky. Serve immediately.

99

Fishy Fishy fish pie

1 sheet ready-made puff pastry

1 egg yolk, beaten

300 g white fish fillets, skinned

300 g smoked fish fillet, skinned

900 ml milk

1 bay leaf

4 hard-boiled eggs, sliced

2 tablespoons vegetable oil

50 g butter

1 onion, finely chopped

1 small carrot, finely chopped

1 celery stick, finely chopped

75 g plain flour

100 g frozen peas, defrosted

200 g prawns, peeled

200 g fresh scallops, cleaned with the roe left on

salt and freshly ground black pepper

Serves 8

A fish pie should be a celebration of the best offcuts of whatever seasonal fish is available, but this is especially so in the winter months when mussels, scallops, cod and plaice are at their best and smoked fish is abundant. This is just as good made with tail fillet offcuts so ask your fishmonger for any cheap fish pieces. Cooking the fish and pastry lid separately is a nice touch as it means you get a perfect pastry topping.

1 Preheat the oven to 180°C/350°F/gas 4. Roll out the puff pastry to a thickness of about 5 mm. Place the dish you will be using for the fish pie upside down on the pastry and cut around the rim. Carefully pull away any unwanted pastry and place the lid on a baking tray lined with greaseproof paper. Brush a little egg yolk over the lid and add any pastry shapes made from the offcuts, if you wish. Brush with egg again and set aside.

2 Put the white and smoked fish in a large frying pan, pour over the milk and add the bay leaf. Poach over a low heat for about 5 minutes until the fish is just cooked. Discard the bay leaf, strain the milk into a jug and set aside. Flake the fish into a large ovenproof pie dish and scatter the hard-boiled eggs evenly over the fish.

3 Heat the oil and butter in a saucepan and slowly sweat the onion, carrot and celery till soft. Stir in the flour and salt and pepper and cook for another 1–2 minutes. Slowly add the reserved poaching milk and bring to the boil. Stir continuously until the sauce thickens. Add the peas, prawns and scallops, stir together and pour over the flaked fish. Place the dish in the oven for 20–25 minutes. After about 5 minutes of cooking time put the pastry lid in the oven (it should take about 15–20 minutes to cook).

4 When the fish pie is hot and bubbling and the pastry is golden and puffed up, remove from the oven and place the lid on top of the dish before serving.

Skate wing with brown butter

2 x 500-g fresh skate wings

100 g flour, seasoned with salt and freshly ground black pepper

beurre noisette (see page 172)

1 tablespoon olive oil, for frying

100 g unsalted butter, for frying

Serves 2

The meaty skate is actually a species of ray. It once featured regularly on fish and chip shop menus but it has declined in popularity over the years, which is probably no bad thing for stocks. Many different types of skate are caught off British shores but ask only for blonde and thornback as they are the most sustainably fished.

1 Preheat the oven to 180°C/350°F/gas 4 and place a baking tray inside. Dust the skate wings with seasoned flour on each side, shaking off any excess, and set aside.

2 Next make the beurre noisette and set aside until needed.

3 Heat the olive oil in frying pan, add the unsalted butter and allow to melt. Add the skate wings and pan-fry for 2 minutes each side then remove and put in the oven on the warmed baking tray for 5 minutes.

4 Remove the skate wings from the oven and allow to rest for a couple of minutes. Pour the beurre noisette over the fish and serve.

Note
The Victorians are said to have banned the landing of whole rays as the fish had large flaps of skin on either side of their tails, which looked a bit like genitals and it was thought they would offend women.

102

Fishy Fishy fish cakes

500 ml fish stock (see page 33),

500 g white fish fillets, such as pollock or whiting

500 g potatoes

20 ml double cream

1 small bunch each of parsley and coriander, chopped

1 egg yolk

1 smoked mackerel fillet

flour, for dusting

1 egg, beaten

200 g fresh breadcrumbs

pomace olive oil
(see note page 71), for frying

salt and freshly ground black pepper

Hollandaise sauce, to serve

Serves 6

Homemade fish cakes are so much better than the shop-bought ones. Use whatever white fish is available. Adding a smoked mackerel fillet to the mix gives them a little more punch.

1 Put the fish stock in a large frying pan and bring to a gentle simmer. Gently place the fillets in the stock and cook for about 6–8 minutes or until cooked through. Remove and allow to cool.

2 Peel the potatoes and boil until soft. Mash with the cream, herbs, egg yolk and some seasoning to make a smooth herby mash.

3 Gently flake the cooled fish fillets and the smoked mackerel fillet together. Combine with the mash and fold the two together, being careful not to break the fish up too much.

4 With floured hands shape the mixture into 6 cakes. Lightly dust each one with flour and then dip in the beaten egg and finally the breadcrumbs. Make sure each one is evenly coated. Chill in the fridge until needed.

5 Preheat the oven to 180°C/350°F/gas 4. Heat the oil in a shallow frying pan. To check the temperature of the oil, throw a pinch of breadcrumbs into the oil: they should start to bubble straight away. If the oil starts to smoke it's too hot so turn off the heat and start again. Shallow-fry the fish cakes for about 5 minutes each side over a gentle heat until browned. Don't worry about the sides looking uncooked or whether the fish cakes are cooked through as this will be done in the oven.

6 Once browned place the fish cakes in an ovenproof dish and cook in the preheated oven for a further 10 minutes. Remove from the oven and drain on kitchen paper to absorb any excess oil. Serve with Hollandaise sauce.

Whole baked lemon sole with a lemon, herb and Parmesan crust

4 x 300–400-g lemon sole, cleaned

olive oil

asparagus, to serve

For the lemon, herb and Parmesan crust

100 g breadcrumbs

rind of 1 lemon, finely chopped

20 g grated Parmesan

4 tablespoons chopped parsley

salt and freshly ground black pepper

Serves 4

Lemon sole is simple but excellent. This crust adds interest and flavour without overwhelming the fish.

1 For the crust, mix the breadcrumbs, the finely chopped lemon rind, Parmesan and chopped parsley with a pinch of salt and pepper in a bowl. Set aside.

2 Preheat the oven to 200°C/400°F/gas 6. Place the whole fish on a lightly oiled baking tray, skin side down. Season with salt and pepper and place in the oven. After about 10 minutes remove from the oven and cover the whole fish with a thin layer of the breadcrumb mix so you can't see any of the white flesh. Return to the oven and cook for a further 10 minutes, or until the crust starts to brown. Do not allow it to go totally brown, just along the top of the fish. Remove and serve with some fresh asparagus.

Quick crab, chilli and basil linguini

175 g dried linguini

2 tablespoons olive oil

½ teaspoon chilli purée

½ teaspoon garlic purée

250 g white crab meat

100 ml white wine

50 g unsalted butter

salt and freshly ground black pepper

fresh basil, to garnish

Serves 2

This pasta dish can be prepared in minutes – for those occasions when you are just too tired to cook an elaborate meal but still want to serve something a little special with minimal effort.

1 Bring a large saucepan of water to the boil, add a good pinch of sea salt and a drizzle of olive oil. Add the linguini and cook for 10 minutes until just al dente, tender but still firm to the bite. Drain in a colander and then refresh under cold running water – this will prevent the pasta from sticking. This can be done a good few hours before needed.

2 Heat the oil in a large frying pan or wok and add the chilli and garlic purées. Add the crab meat, white wine, butter and seasoning and mix gently to combine. Add the cooked linguini and stir to heat through. Serve in a large pasta bowl with torn basil leaves sprinkled on top.

Note
The beauty of this dish is that the pasta can be cooked beforehand, which is a great time-saver. If you like more – or less – heat, increase or reduce the amount of chilli purée.

Seafood risotto

300 g cooked shell-on North Atlantic prawns

1 litre fish stock

2 tablespoons olive oil

1 white onion, finely chopped

2 garlic cloves, crushed

300 g arborio risotto rice

12 mussels, scrubbed and beards removed

150 g white fish fillets

chopped fresh parsley and Parmesan shavings, to serve

salt and freshly ground black pepper

Serves 4

Risotto is a simple, everyday dish which is easy to make. It takes time – you have to stand over it and slowly stir in the liquid bit by bit but it's almost therapeutic. You can add chicken or vegetables of your choice to flavour it, but a seafood risotto is both healthy and impressive.

1 Peel all but a handful of the prawns and set aside. Place the stock in a saucepan and bring to a gentle simmer.

2 Heat the oil in a large saucepan and gently cook the onion, taking care not to colour too much. This will take about 10 minutes. Add the garlic and stir through for 1–2 minutes. Add the rice and fry for a few minutes or until each grain of rice is coated in the oil. Slowly add the fish stock a couple of ladles at a time, gently stirring so the vegetables soften and the stock is absorbed by the rice. Keep adding more stock at intervals until the rice is just tender, keeping back a couple of ladles of stock. Each addition of stock should be absorbed before you add the next instalment.

3 Discard any mussels that fail to close when tapped sharply. Add the fish, mussels and prawns (peeled and unpeeled) and remaining stock into the saucepan and cover. Cook for 5–10 minutes over very low heat, making sure the fish is cooked through and the mussels open. Discard any mussels that fail to open. The rice should be plump, tender and creamy. Serve with shaved Parmesan and season.

Red mullet salad with sauce vierge

1 tablespoon olive oil

15 g butter

8 red mullet fillets

4 handfuls mixed salad leaves

1 small red onion, sliced

sauce vierge (see page 174), to serve

Serves 4

Red mullet is a very colourful fish which makes for an excellent salad, served with warm sauce vierge.

1 Heat a frying pan until hot and add the olive oil and butter. When the butter starts foaming place the mullet skin side down in the pan and cook slowly until the skin goes crispy.

2 Divide the salad leaves and sliced onion among 4 plates and place the cooked fillets skin side up on top. Finish by drizzling some warm sauce vierge around the edges of the plates.

Fish and prawn curry

1 teaspoon cumin seeds

1 teaspoon coriander seeds

1 small onion, finely chopped

1 garlic clove, crushed

1 lemongrass stalk, finely chopped

1 green chilli, deseeded and finely chopped

1 x 5-cm piece root ginger, peeled and very finely chopped

1 small green pepper, deseeded and finely chopped

2 tablespoons fish sauce

2 x 400-ml tins coconut milk

400 g white fish fillets, such as plaice, pollock or whiting, cut into bite-sized pieces

200 g cooked prawns

1 bunch chopped coriander

poppadoms, to serve

Serves 4

This Thai-inspired curry is easy and quick to make. Gently spiced, it adds interest to a weekday menu.

1 Place the cumin and coriander seeds in a frying pan and gently heat for a few minutes until they start to darken. Remove and transfer to a food processor and process until they start to break up. Add the chopped onion, garlic, lemongrass, chilli, ginger, and green pepper to the cumin and coriander and continue to process, gently adding small amounts of fish sauce until you have a thick and smooth paste.

2 Gently warm a frying pan and add the paste. Cook over a very low heat (you do not want to burn it) for a couple of minutes and then add the coconut milk.

3 When you are ready to serve simply put the curry sauce into a saucepan and bring gently to the boil. Add the fish pieces and cook for 5 minutes, or until the fish turns opaque and firms up. Add the prawns and heat through. Place in a bowl, sprinkle over some fresh coriander and serve with poppadoms.

Bream fillets with couscous and citrus salsa

These bream fillets are served on a bed of couscous with a citrus salsa on the side. Salsas add variety and freshness to a dish, and only take a minute to prepare.

4 wild bream fillets

citrus salsa (see page 173), to serve

olive oil, for frying

butter, for frying

For the couscous

350 ml vegetable stock

150 g couscous

1 teaspoon chopped parsley

1 teaspoon chopped basil

1 teaspoon chopped chervil

1 teaspoon lemon juice

1 teaspoon lemon zest

Serves 2

1 First make the salsa and chill in the fridge until needed.

2 Make the couscous. Bring the vegetable stock to the boil in a small pan. Place the couscous in a bowl and pour over the hot stock. Whisk briefly and then cover with cling film. Leave for about 5 minutes or until all the stock is absorbed. Stir in the herbs, lemon juice and zest and then fluff up with a fork. Allow to cool.

3 Heat the oil and butter in a large frying pan. When the butter is foaming place the bream fillets skin side down in the pan, pressing down on the flesh lightly so the fillets don't curl. After 1–2 minutes, or when the fillets start to turn pale, turn them over and cook for a further few minutes.

4 Remove the fillets and place under a hot grill to finish off. Arrange the fillets skin side up on a bed of couscous and drizzle the citrus salsa around the fillets to serve.

Note
You can cheat on this salsa quite easily with a drained can of tinned tomatoes in the cold winter months, but nothing quite beats making any salsa with your own home-grown or at least market-bought, local tomatoes in the summer.

Pan-fried plaice fillets with sauce vierge

sauce vierge (see page 174)

1 tablespoon olive oil

25 g butter

2 plaice fillets

75 g mixed salad leaves

10 g sliced red onion

Serves 2

The best time to eat plaice is from summer to midwinter. It is best avoided early in the year when the fish are spawning and full of roe and just after the spawning time, when they are regaining their strength.

1 First make the sauce vierge and set aside until needed.

2 Put the olive oil and butter in a large frying pan and heat until the butter starts foaming. Add the plaice fillets, skin side down and cook until the skin goes crispy.

3 Place the salad leaves and the sliced red onion in a large bowl and arrange the plaice fillets skin side up on top, with warm sauce vierge drizzled over them.

Grilled lemon sole with salsa verde

1 medium lemon sole, trimmed

olive oil

salt and pepper

new potatoes, to serve

salsa verde (see page 173), to serve

Serves 1

The sole here is served simply with salsa verde, so as not to detract from the quality of the fish.

1 First make the salsa verde and set aside until needed.

2 Preheat the oven to 200°C/400°F/gas 6. Place the lemon sole on a piece of oiled and seasoned parchment paper dark side down and bake in the oven for 12–15 minutes. When the flesh starts to go firm remove the sole from the oven and place it under a hot grill for about 2–3 minutes. When it has gone a little darker serve with new potatoes and the salsa verde drizzled over the top of the fish.

Spicy crab

2 whole crabs, cooked

50 ml olive oil

25 g butter

2 shallots, finely chopped

100 ml white wine

1 x 1-cm piece of fresh ginger, peeled and chopped

For the chilli purée

4 garlic cloves, crushed

3 green chillies, deseeded and chopped

1 tablespoon olive oil

Serves 2

This is a great way to serve crab but you will need a large pan. You could also cook the crabs one at a time.

1 Prepare the crab (see page 55), remove all the dark meat from the head and set aside. Leave the white meat in the body and legs. Remove and crack the claws and set aside.

2 To make the chilli purée put the garlic cloves and chillies in a food processor and process until you have a paste (add olive oil if necessary).

3 Heat the butter and oil in a large pan (the largest you have) and add the shallot. Cook gently until translucent, about 4–5 minutes and then add the white wine and bring to the boil. Add about a tablespoon of the chilli purée and stir through, then add the chopped ginger and the crab claws and coat with the liquid. Add the brown meat and the rest of the body and shell. Cover and allow to steam for 4 minutes. Give the pan another good stir to coat as much of the shell as possible .

4 Arrange the main body of the crab and the claws in a bowl and top off with the shell. Pour the remaining juice from the saucepan over the crab. Serve with a crab cracker, picker and soup spoon for the sauce.

Mussels (three ways)

People are often put off mussels because they think, quite wrongly, that they are difficult to prepare and cook. Take care when cleaning and preparing the mussels (see page 25) and the rest is easy. All recipes serve 1 as a main course, or 2 as a starter.

Moules marinière

800 g live mussels, cleaned
50 ml white wine
50 g shallots, finely diced
2 garlic cloves, crushed
25 g unsalted butter
1 tablespoon chopped parsley
salt and freshly ground black pepper

1 Tip the mussels into a large hot saucepan with the white wine, shallot and garlic. Cover and shake the pan until the mussels start to open. Add the butter and seasoning and shake the pan again. Discard any mussels that remain tightly closed. Serve in a bowl and sprinkle the parsley on top.

Thai-style mussels

800 g live mussels, cleaned
25 ml white wine
50 g shallots, finely diced
1 tablespoon green or red Thai curry paste
50 ml coconut milk
1 tablespoon chopped coriander
salt and freshly ground black pepper

1 Tip the mussels into a large hot saucepan with the white wine, shallot and Thai curry paste (red is hotter than green). Cover and shake the pan until the mussels start to open. Add the coconut milk and seasoning and shake the pan again. Discard any mussels that remain tightly closed. Serve in a bowl and sprinkle the coriander on top.

Provençal-style mussels

800 g live mussels, cleaned
50 g shallots, finely diced
1 garlic clove, crushed
50 ml white wine
1 teaspoon chopped rosemary
25 g unsalted butter
1 small tomato, skinned, deseeded and diced
1 tablespoon chopped parsley
salt and freshly ground black pepper

1 Tip the mussels into a large hot saucepan with the shallots, garlic, white wine and rosemary. Cover and shake the pan until the mussels start to open. Add the butter and seasoning then shake the pan again. Discard any mussels that remain tightly closed. Serve in a bowl and sprinkle the diced tomato and the parsley on top.

Whole roasted grey gurnard

Grey gurnard may be an ugly fish but it has a beautiful secret. It has a very thick, meaty spine which is easy to fillet. Secondly, it feeds on crabs, prawns and other shellfish so has a wonderful seafood flavour. The larger ones turn up in the early spring.

1 x 800-g grey gurnard, cleaned

salt and freshly ground black pepper

mixed salad leaves, to serve

salsa verde (see page 173), to serve

Serves 2

1 Remove the fins from either the side of the head, the spine and the tail. Slice across each side of the fish down to the bone. Season inside and out.

2 Preheat the oven to 180°C/350°F/gas 4 and lightly oil a baking tray. Place the fish on the baking tray and cook in the oven for 30 minutes. Slicing through the fish before cooking speeds up the cooking process.

3 Once cooked simply remove and allow to rest for a few minutes. Serve with a few mixed salad leaves and some salsa verde.

Garlic and herb scallops in the shell

2 garlic cloves, crushed

¼ bunch parsley, chopped

100 g unsalted butter, softened

8 scallops

salt and freshly ground black pepper

Serves 2

Scallops are a fabulous seafood – meaty and delicious. This garlic and herb butter is easy to prepare and is the perfect accompaniment.

1 First make the garlic and herb butter. Mix the crushed garlic and chopped parsley into the butter. Roll into a sausage shape, wrap in greaseproof paper and chill in the fridge.

2 Scallops are often sold already cleaned and removed from their shells, which a fishmonger will often give you for free if you ask nicely. If you find whole scallops still in their shells then cleaning and preparing them is very simple. Shuck the scallops with a sharp knife, cutting the main muscle that holds the shells together. Throw away the flat top and you will see the scallop with the roe attached surrounded by some dirty flesh. Simply cut under the scallop and it will come away from the shell. Remove and discard the rest. Cut off any dark bits of the scallop and pull away any tendons. Whether you keep the roe (the orange bit) is a personal taste.

3 Place the scallop in the shell with a small pat of the garlic and herb butter on top, repeat with the remaining scallops and place on a baking tray. Place under a hot grill and cook for about 5 minutes until the butter starts spitting and the edges of the shell start to darken. Remove the tray, taking care as the shells will be hot, and place on a dish. Season and serve.

Seafood-stuffed squid

1 tablespoon olive oil

1 small onion, chopped

1 carrot, finely chopped

50 g frozen peas

50 g arborio risotto rice

200 ml hot fish stock
(see page 33)

1 x 600-g whole squid, cleaned
and tentacles reserved

50 g cooked shell-on prawns

Serves 2

Fresh local squid is available around the country all through the year. They can get large in the winter, which works well for this recipe. You want the body to remain whole so it will hold the rest of the ingredients.

1 Heat the oil in a large pan and add the onion. Cook until soft and then add the finely chopped carrot and the peas. Cook until the carrot takes on some colour, then add the rice and allow it absorb the oil and the flavour of the vegetables. Add the fish stock, about a tablespoon at a time, until the rice is cooked, about 20 minutes. Set aside.

2 Cut the squid tentacles into 2-cm pieces and pan-fry over a high heat for about 20 seconds, remove from the heat and add to the vegetables and rice. Peel the prawns, add to the rice and mix through. Allow to cool slightly.

3 Preheat the oven to 220°C/425°F/gas 7. Fill as much of the squid head with the rice mixture while still being able to close the opening. Thread a cocktail stick through the end to keep the filling in. Place on a baking tray lined with greaseproof paper and bake in the oven for 5 minutes. Once browned remove from the oven, remove the cocktail stick and serve thickly sliced.

125

Isle of Wight octopus

1 x 400-g whole octopus, cleaned

700 g vine-ripened tomatoes,
cut in half and deseeded

3 garlic cloves, crushed

3 tablespoons olive oil

1 red onion, chopped

2 carrots, finely chopped

75 ml red wine

300 ml fish stock
(see page 33)

1 bay leaf

Serves 2

There are three ways of tenderizing octopus. One is to bash it with a mallet, which makes the slightly tough skin more edible. Another is to freeze it overnight. The final method is to slow-cook it for 3–4 hours. This recipe uses the latter, our preferred method.

1 Cut your prepared octopus into large chunks, including the tentacles. Preheat the oven to 180°C/350°F/gas 4.

2 Place the tomatoes in a roasting dish with the crushed garlic and 2 tablespoons of the oil and roast in the oven for 20 minutes until soft. Reduce the oven temperature to 110°C/225°F/gas ½.

3 Heat the remaining oil in a frying pan and cook the onion until soft. Then add the carrot and cook through. Pour over the red wine and after it calms down pour in the fish stock and reduce for a few minutes. Remove the roasted tomatoes and put through a sieve to remove the skin and garlic and create a smooth passata.

4 Put the sieved tomatoes back into the roasting tray and add the fish stock, bay leaf and vegetable mixture. Finally add the chopped octopus head and tentacles and return to the oven. Cook on a low heat for 3 hours, checking and stirring regularly. If it starts to look a little dry add some more fish stock or wine. Discard the bay leaf before serving.

Note
We always thought that the nearest octopus to us was in the Mediterranean. So it came as some surprise when a fish supplier called up and asked if we wanted some Isle of Wight octopus. Sure enough a couple of hours later the kitchen was standing around sorting through a few kilos of local octopus wondering what recipe to use. So yes, if you live near the island then you may get lucky otherwise any fresh eight-armed cephalopod will do.

Monkfish scampi with sweet cider sauce

2 eggs, beaten

flour, for dusting

breadcrumbs
(Japanese if possible)

600 g monkfish tail fillet,
cut into bite-sized chunks

oil, for deep-frying

For the sweet cider sauce

20 ml olive oil

25 g butter

2 banana shallots, finely chopped

2 garlic cloves, crushed

1 sprig of thyme

250 ml sweet cider

250 ml double cream

1 tablespoon chopped parsley

salt and freshly ground black
pepper

Serves 4

Monkfish is a deep-water fish with a massive ugly head and a long tail. This is where the flesh is and is often why you only find the tails on sale. They are very easy to fillet as there is just one central spine.

1 First make the cider sauce. Heat the olive oil and butter in a pan and sweat the shallots over a medium heat until softened. Add the garlic, thyme and cider and cook until reduced by two thirds. Add the cream and gently simmer until the sauce thickens, about 5 minutes. Season to taste and remove from the heat. Add the chopped parsley and set aside.

2 Whisk the eggs in a bowl. Sift the flour on to a plate and but the breadcrumbs in a bowl. Take a piece of the monkfish, dust in the flour, then dip in the egg and then the breadcrumbs. Swirl the monkfish around in the breadcrumbs until covered on all sides and then set aside. Heat the oil in a wok or deep-fat fryer to a temperature of 180°C/350°F and drop the scampi into the hot oil, a few at a time. Cook for about 5 minutes until brown.

3 The sauce can be served warm or cold. If preferred, gently reheat the sweet cider sauce and then pour into a ramekin or dipping bowl. Serve with the scampi.

Note
Japanese breadcrumbs are ideal for deep-frying fish and seafood. They can be found in any good supermarket and provide a light coating which complements fish and seafood.

John Dory en papillotte

8 John Dory fillets

150 g unsalted butter

200 g wild mushrooms

100 g spinach

200 ml single cream

salt and freshly ground black pepper

Serves 4

Cooking the fish fillets in a paper parcel seals ensures that none of the flavour is lost.

1 Season the fish with salt and pepper and set aside. Cut four squares of greaseproof paper, approximately 20 x 20 cm.

2 Melt the butter in a pan and add the mushrooms. Fry for about 5 minutes, add the spinach and stir gently for 1–2 minutes until the spinach has wilted. Add the cream and set aside.

3 Preheat the oven to 200°C/400°F/gas 6. Place the fillets individually in a rectangle of greaseproof paper and spoon a couple of tablespoons of the cream and spinach sauce on top. Fold all the sides of the paper parcels together to seal. Bake in the oven for 10 minutes. Gently remove the parcels and put directly on the plate.

Note

John Dory is a fish revered by fish lovers across the British south coast. The spots on either side are said to be the thumb and finger print of St Peter, the fishing disciple, who marked the fish when he picked it from the sea. It's quite a solitary fish and only really gets as far as the English Channel so it's not actively fished for and is often a by-catch in summer. So it may be rare and you will probably have to pay a little more than for your normal fish choice. But it's a good-tasting holy fish so maybe it's worth it.

Baked plaice with garlic and thyme new potatoes

1 x 600-g whole plaice, cleaned

salt and freshly ground black pepper

For the potatoes

200 g new potatoes, scrubbed

1 tablespoon olive oil

2 whole garlic bulbs

3–4 sprigs thyme

salt and freshly ground black pepper

Serves 1

The garlic and thyme flavouring of the new potatoes is very subtle, and goes very well with the plaice.

1 Score through the skin of the fish on both sides and season with salt and pepper. Set aside. Preheat the oven to 200°C/400°F/gas 6.

2 Cook the new potatoes in a saucepan of boiling salted water for 10 minutes. Drain and place in an ovenproof dish with the olive oil, salt and pepper and toss to coat. Cut the whole garlic bulbs in half and place among the potatoes together with the thyme sprigs. Roast in the oven for 20 minutes.

3 Meanwhile, line a separate baking tray with lightly oiled greaseproof paper and put the plaice on top. Bake in the oven for 10–15 minutes.

4 Remove the roasting tray containing the potatoes and push down on the garlic to release some of the cooked cloves and make a paste. Remove the remaining garlic and stir in the hot garlic paste to the cooking juices. Remove the whole plaice and serve whole with the new potatoes in a separate bowl.

Monkfish wrapped in Parma ham

2 courgettes, cut into chunks

1 large red onion

2 yellow peppers

6 firm plum tomatoes

300 g baby new potatoes

3 tablespoons olive oil

8 slices Parma ham

4 x150-g monkfish tail fillets

salt and freshly ground black pepper

Serves 4

This is a quick but elegant dish to prepare, for when you feel like a midweek treat.

1 Preheat the oven to 200°C/400°F/gas 6. Cut the courgettes, onion and peppers into large chunks and halve the tomatoes. Place in a large roasting tray with the new potatoes, olive oil and seasoning and toss to coat completely in the oil. Place in the oven and cook for about 30 minutes, until the vegetables are just tender.

2 Meanwhile, wrap the Parma ham slices round the monkfish fillets and ensure they are completely covered. Pan-fry for 1–2 minutes until brown all over. You are not cooking the fish, just sealing it. Remove and place on baking tray and cook in the oven for 15–18 minutes.

3 Serve with the roasted vegetables.

132

Fishy Fishy fish and chips

A classic British dish, proper fish and chips are hard to beat. A good batter is essential.

2 large floury potatoes

2 tablespoons olive oil

225 g plain flour, plus extra for rolling

1 teaspoon baking powder

½ teaspoon salt

300 ml local ale or lager

2 x 150-g white fish fillets

oil, for deep-frying

mushy peas (see page 177), lemon wedges and tartare sauce (see page 166), to serve

Serves 2

1 Scrub and peel the potatoes and cut into thick chips (leave unpeeled if you like a more rustic chip). Bring a large pan of salted water to the boil and cook the chips for 2–3 minutes. Drain thoroughly and then tip into a roasting tray. Drizzle over the oil and give the tray a shake to cover the chips. Cook in the oven for 30 minutes, turning occasionally.

2 Put the flour, baking powder and salt into a bowl and whisk in the beer until you have a smooth batter. Dust the fish fillets in flour and then place them in the batter, ensuring they are completely covered, then pull them up the side of the bowl to remove any excess batter.

3 Heat the oil in a deep-fat fryer to 180°C/350°F. Alternatively heat the oil in a large wok – it's the right temperature when a cube of bread turns golden brown in 30 seconds. Do take care when heating large quantities of oil at home. Cook the fillets for about 5–8 minutes, until golden brown. Remove from the oil and place on kitchen paper to absorb any excess oil. Serve with the chips, mushy peas, lemon wedges and some homemade tartare sauce.

Lemon sole stuffed with ratatouille

4 x 500–600-g lemon sole

salt and freshly ground black pepper

new potatoes, buttered, to serve

seasonal vegetables, to serve

For the ratatouille

25 ml olive oil

25 g butter

3 red peppers, diced

2 courgettes, diced

1 aubergine, diced

2 large tomatoes, diced

1 tablespoon tomato purée

1 tablespoon garlic purée

2 teaspoons hot smoked paprika

Serves 4

This is a speedy dish to prepare for a special midweek meal at home.

1 Preheat the oven to 180°/350°F/gas 4. Make the ratatouille. Heat the olive oil and butter in a saucepan and cook all the diced vegetables over a medium heat for 15 minutes. Stir in the tomato and garlic purées, together with the paprika and allow to cool.

2 Place the sole, flesh side down, on a counter and, using a sharp filleting knife, cut a line down the dorsal spine from just behind the head to just above the tail. Angle the knife at 45° towards the edge of the fish and slowly pass the knife between the flesh and the bones, as if you were removing a fillet. Stop when you are a few centimetres from the edge (skirt). Turn the fish around and repeat, starting at the tail, to create 2 pouches.

3 Stuff the ratatouille into the pouch until it is plump. Repeat with the other fish.

4 Place one or two seasoned baking trays in the preheated oven. When warm, lay the fish carefully on top and bake for about 12–15 minutes, until the flesh is firm and the ratatouille begins to turn golden brown.

5 Remove from the oven and serve with buttered new potatoes and seasonal vegetables.

Fish goujons with lemon crème fraîche

600 g plaice or pollock fillets

flour, for dusting

2 eggs, beaten

200 g breadcrumbs

oil, for deep-frying

lemon crème fraîche
(see page 167)

Serves 2

Fish goujons have fallen slightly from favour, which is a pity as they are not very complicated to make and lend themselves to being served with a variety of delicious dips, such as the lemon crème fraîche suggested here, or a flavoured mayonnaise of your choice. Time for a revival!

1 Cut the fish into 5-cm strips. Sift the flour on to a plate, put the beaten eggs in a bowl and the breadcrumbs into a salad bowl. Your fish goujon production line is ready.

2 Take a strip of fish, place it in the flour and cover evenly, then dip it into the beaten egg to cover, gently shaking off any excess. Dip the goujons in breadcrumbs. Gently swirl the bowl to cover the goujons evenly then remove with tongs.

3 Either place the goujons immediately in oil in a hot deep-fryer or fry in a frying pan in about 1 cm oil. If you do not want to eat them straight away, the goujons can be put on a clean plate and frozen (there will be no need to thaw, as they can easily be cooked from frozen). Put a couple of goujons in the pan or fryer and cook until golden brown, about 5 minutes each side. Remove and place on kitchen paper to absorb any excess oil. Serve with the lemon crème fraîche.

Special occasions

The best Bloody Mary

170 ml tomato juice

1 shot vodka

1 teaspoon horseradish sauce

pinch of paprika

Tabasco, to taste

1–2 teaspoons Worcestershire sauce, or to taste

½ shot port

1 shot Tio Pepe sherry

pinch of celery salt

freshly ground black pepper

1 x 20-cm celery stick, topped and tailed, to serve

1 oyster, to serve

Serves 1

From the classic repertoire of cocktails, often served with brunch, Bloody Mary is the perfect partner to fish dishes.

1 Put the tomato juice, vodka, horseradish, paprika and as much or as little Tabasco as you like into a cocktail shaker, fill with ice and stir (don't shake or the tomato juice will go frothy). This is your basic Bloody Mary mix.

2 To serve, put 3 ice cubes in a glass and put the Worcestershire sauce in the bottom. Add the Bloody Mary mix, filling the glass to within 1 cm of the rim. Add the port.

3 Clean out the cocktail shaker and put in some more ice, add the Tio Pepe and shake until the shaker is almost too cold to hold. Pour the sherry into the top of the glass so it creates a thin clear layer. Finish with a pinch of celery salt and a couple of grinds from a pepper mill. Cut a small slit in the celery stick and put on the side of the glass. Serve with a straw and the oyster on the side.

Note

Every barman has his own version of this classic cocktail. The ice-cold sherry provides a perfect hit of alcohol before the refreshing Bloody Mary mix. Port is a newer ingredient which gives a slight twist to the classic recipe.

Pan-fried sea bass fillets with black olive tapenade

olive oil, for frying

butter, for frying

4 sea bass fillets

salt and freshly ground black pepper

For the tapenade

2 anchovy fillets

100 g pitted black olives

2 garlic cloves

1 tablespoon capers

juice of ½ lemon

1 tablespoon olive oil

Serves 2

Sea bass fillets make an elegant but easy to cook main course. The black olive tapenade adds a robust flavour to the dish.

1 Make the tapenade. Put all the ingredients in a food processor and blend until you have a paste. Add a little more oil if the paste is too thick. Set aside.

2 Put some olive oil and a little butter in a large hot frying pan. Season the fillets on both sides with salt and pepper and when the butter starts to foam add the fillets skin side down. Reduce the heat to medium and after 3 minutes, or when the flesh starts to turn white, turn the fillets over skin side up and cook for a further minute.

3 Remove the fish from the pan and then add a tablespoon of the tapenade to the hot pan. Stir into the juices in the pan and then drizzle the warm tapenade over the fish. Serve immediately.

Mixed fish platter with roasted new potatoes

1 kg new potatoes, scrubbed

olive oil, for roasting

2 large sprigs rosemary

4–5 whole fish, such as sea bass, wild sea bream or pink gurnard, cleaned and gutted but left whole

a few bay leaves

300 g mussels, scrubbed

1 onion, sliced

150 ml fish stock (see page 33)

125 ml white wine

Serves 4–6

This is an excellent party dish. Serve the mixed fish platter in the centre of the table and allow your guests to help themselves. Ask your fishmonger for smaller whole fish.

1 Preheat the oven to 200°C/400°F/gas 6. Parboil the potatoes for about 10 minutes in some salted water. Drain and place in an ovenproof dish with some olive oil and rosemary and roast in the oven for about 15 minutes. Shake the dish occasionally.

2 If not already done, cut off all the fins from the fish and remove the gills. Make diagonal slashes in the skin of each fish with a sharp knife, taking care not to cut too deeply, and place a bay leaf in each one. Arrange the fish on the largest ovenproof dish you have, add the sliced onions and mussels and pour over the fish stock. Cover with foil and reduce the oven temperature to 180°C/350°F/gas 4. Place the fish in the oven, ideally above the potatoes and cook for about 25 minutes. Check if the fish is cooked – the flesh should be opaque and feel firm to the touch. Return to the oven for a further 5 minutes if necessary. Check the potatoes are browned and remove to serve.

3 Remove the whole fish from the ovenproof dish and place on the largest serving platter or metal tray you have. It doesn't matter if the fish overlap. Stir the white wine into the fish stock in the roasting dish. If it is a ceramic ovenproof dish there will be enough heat to cook off the alcohol. Pour the liquid over the fish, making sure each fish is well covered. Arrange the roasted potatoes on the platter, ideally sitting in the fish juice, some of which they will soak up.

4 Serve the platter in the centre of the table and let everyone help themselves.

141

Cod with champ and kale

4 x 250-g thick cod fillets

4 handfuls winter kale, shredded

100 g unsalted butter

juice of ½ lemon

salt and freshly ground black pepper

For the champ

1 kg potatoes

125 g unsalted butter

100 ml double cream

salt and white pepper

100 g spring onions, sliced

Serves 4

The main thing you need to know about cod is that it is seasonal. It likes cold, choppy waters so goes wherever it can find them. Therefore it is found around the British inshore coast in the winter and moves to deeper, colder water in the summer. So if you eat cod all year round then you are not giving the stocks time to recover from being fished (see pages 18–21).

1 First make the champ (or spring onion mash). Peel the potatoes and boil until soft. Drain well and mash. Add the cream and butter and stir vigorously until smooth (less if you prefer a chunkier mash). Season with salt and white pepper. Fold the spring onions into the mash and keep warm while you cook the fish.

2 Preheat the grill to high and lightly oil a baking tray. Place the cod fillet on it, skin side down and grill for 5 minutes. Meanwhile, bring a pan of salted water to the boil. Turn the cod fillet skin side up and continue to grill under a high heat. Drop the kale into the boiling water and cook for 2–3 minutes. Drain and toss with half the butter and the lemon juice. Season to taste.

3 Once the cod skin is brown at the edges remove the fillets and serve on top of the buttered kale. Top each fillet with the rest of the butter and serve with the champ.

142

Lobsterfest

Lobster is generally accepted to be the king of shellfish; flown thousands of miles around the world every day, courted by the haves and worshipped by the have-nots. It is adored by chefs and foodies alike and has added a touch of luxury to countless recipes. However, some would say the best way to eat a lobster is the simplest – freshly boiled and served with garlic butter or mayonnaise.

Lobsters can't be farmed and can only be caught wild. They are fiercely territorial and despite the rumours that they mate for life, they will quite happily attack and eat each other and their young given the chance. Around the British coast lobsters are seasonal. From late autumn they head for deeper waters, too deep for them to be caught. For this reason you won't be able to buy British lobsters between November and March. The best time to get local lobster is during July and August when they are cheap and bountiful. In North America, Maine has cornered the market in year-round lobster, as they do not venture very far. So if you are eating a lobster in winter it has probably been flown in live from Maine. This makes them expensive, a price tag which lobster lovers seem prepared to pay.

So why has the lobster been placed on this pedestal? The answer can lie in one word, Lobsterfest. A lobster is simply more festive and luxurious than a crab and can bring sheer delight and amusement to your friends and family sitting on a large table, covered in newspaper because it's going to get messy. In front of you lies a grilled lobster, a pile of golden fries, a cold glass of Sauvignon Blanc and an afternoon of laughter and conversation as everybody picks and sucks their way through every bit of meat they can. Lobsters make people smile, a priceless quality.

There are many views on the most humane way to kill a lobster. Certainly, the quickest method, a knife straight through the head, is often the messiest. If you want to eat the best lobster then you are going to have to accept that you will be responsible for killing it. A pre-cooked lobster left to cool and then reheated is not worth the investment you have already made in it. The cleanest option is to put the live lobster in a freezer for 20 minutes, which makes it very docile, and then plunge it into a large pan of boiling salted water and cook for about 15–20 minutes until the shell turns bright red. Any movement after that will just be a reaction of the nervous system.

Grilled lobster

1 x 600–800-g lobster, freshly killed

50 g garlic and herb butter (see page 172), cut in pats

mixed salad leaves, lemon wedges and french fries, to serve

Serves 1–2

1 Remove the claws and split the lobster in half lengthways. Pull away the grey spongy gills and the stomach sac from the top of the head and discard.

2 Put the garlic and herb butter pats on a baking tray and put the lobster halves flesh side down on top. Grill until the lobster starts to colour, about 5 minutes, then turn the halves over and place them back under the grill for another 1–2 minutes.

3 Serve with mixed salad leaves, lemon wedges and french fries. Drizzle any butter left on the tray over the lobster.

Lobster linguini

1 x 600–800-g lobster,
live or freshly boiled

300-g packet dried linguini

2 tablespoons olive oil

10 g unsalted butter

1 onion, finely chopped

2 garlic cloves, crushed

1 x 400-g tin tomatoes

8–10 fresh basil leaves

Serves 4

This pasta dish is simple but very luxurious. It is guaranteed to be loved by lobster lovers everywhere.

1 Kill the lobster by putting it in the freezer for 20 minutes, which makes it very docile. Then plunge into boiling water and boil for 10 minutes. Allow to cool. If it is already boiled just give it a wash. Twist off the claws and remove the legs. Using shellfish crackers, crack the claws and legs and pull out the meat.

2 Place the lobster tail on a board and cut in half along its length with a sharp knife. Remove the thin grey vein of intestine running along its length. Remove the meat from the tail. Carefully lift out the bony part of the head and break into pieces. Pick out as much flesh as you can. Pull away the grey spongy gills and stomach sac from the top of the head and discard. Keep all the shells to one side.

3 Once all the meat is out make the lobster stock. On a good chopping board, chop the shell, legs and any other part into small sizes, enough to fit into your saucepan. Cover with water and boil for 20 minutes then remove as much meat off the shell as you can and drain the stock into a bowl. Wipe the saucepan and put the lobster stock back into the saucepan and leave on a rolling boil until it has reduced.

4 Cook the linguini until al dente. Drain, stir in a tablespoon of olive oil and set aside.

5 Melt the butter in a frying pan, add a little olive oil and the chopped onion. Cook gently for a few minutes then add the crushed garlic and continue to cook until the onions soften. Empty the tin of tomatoes into a fine-meshed or conical sieve and stir gently, pressing the tomatoes through the sieve into the pan. This will allow all the juice

to pass through but leave the seeds and pulp behind, basically creating an easy passata. Heat gently until cooked through, add a couple of fresh basil leaves and set aside.

6 Once the lobster stock has reduced by about half stir it into the tomato sauce. For a stronger flavour allow the stock to reduce down to a third.

7 Chop the lobster meat into chunks as evenly as you can. The meat is very rich so you don't want huge amounts. The sauce will flavour the linguini.

8 When you are ready to serve place a ladleful of the lobster sauce into a frying pan over a gentle heat. Add a portion of the linguini and stir in, once warmed through, add a quarter of the lobster meat and again heat through. Once hot tip into a pasta bowl and keep warm while you repeat with the other 3 portions. Top with a few more torn basil leaves and serve.

Lobster Thermidor

1 x 800–900-g crippled lobster

25 g breadcrumbs

mixed salad leaves, to serve

For the sauce

50 g unsalted butter

1 shallot, finely chopped

2 garlic cloves, crushed

1 teaspoon English mustard

25 ml white wine

1 teaspoon paprika

125 ml double cream

100 g freshly grated Parmesan

1 sprig tarragon, chopped

Serves 2

This is a classic recipe and one which is synonymous with luxury. Ask your fishmonger if he has any crippled lobsters – lobsters often lose one of their claws to fights and will grow new ones, a process which takes a year or so. They can't be sold whole so are often much cheaper than their two-clawed friends. What you lose in a claw you often make up in size as you can buy a larger lobster for the same money.

1 Plunge the live lobster in boiling water and cook for 15 minutes. Allow to cool, split in half and discard the stomach sac, gills and intestine (see page 150). Remove all the meat except for that from the legs. Rinse the shell halves and dry with kitchen paper. Chop the meat into bite-sized chunks and set aside.

2 Make the sauce. Melt the butter in a saucepan and gently cook the shallot, without allowing it to burn. As it starts to soften add the crushed garlic and cook through. Stir in the mustard, mixing well, then add the white wine and heat through. Add the paprika and double cream and stir in again. Do not allow the sauce to boil – just keep it over a low heat. Add two thirds of the Parmesan and tarragon and stir gently until it forms a thick sauce. Remove from the heat, add the lobster meat and evenly coat it with the sauce.

3 Fill the lobster shells with the mixture. Mix the remaining Parmesan with the breadcrumbs and gently sprinkle over the lobster. Place under a hot grill until the mixture is bubbling and the breadcrumbs are browned. Remove and serve with salad leaves.

153

Grilled oysters

2 dozen size 2 rock oysters

1 lemon, quartered

Tabasco, to taste

Oysters Rockefeller

4 teaspoons melted butter

25 g breadcrumbs

1 spring onion, finely sliced

8 baby spinach leaves,
sliced thinly

Tabasco, to taste

1 teaspoon chopped parsley

Oysters Mornay

2 tablespoons white sauce
(made with butter, flour and milk)

50 g mature Cheddar, grated

freshly ground black pepper

Oysters Kilpatrick

4 teaspoons melted butter

2 unsmoked bacon rashers, grilled
and sliced into small pieces

Worcestershire sauce

freshly ground black pepper

Oysters with ginger and soy

1 x 1-cm piece root ginger, grated

1 spring onion, finely sliced

soy sauce

sesame oil

freshly ground black pepper

Serves 4

This is a great dish to do for friends who love oysters. The idea is that every person gets two raw oysters, and one each of the prepared oysters.

1 Arrange all the ingredients so they are near to you. Shuck all 24 oysters (see page 46) and put 12 of them on a baking tray. Lay the oysters on a bed of coarse salt if they are wobbling around too much. Set the remaining 12 oysters aside.

2 Then, using a teaspoon, layer 4 of the oysters on the baking tray with the Rockefeller ingredients, 4 with the Mornay ingredients and 4 with the Kilpatrick ingredients.

3 Top 4 of the remaining oysters with the ginger and soy ingredients and leave the remaining 8 as they are.

4 Put the baking tray under a hot grill and cook until the oysters start to bubble. Remove and serve with the eight uncooked oysters plus the four ginger and soy oysters, some lemon wedges and a few drops of Tabasco.

154

A very British fruits de mer platter

crushed ice

1 x 600-g cooked lobster

1 x 500-g cooked crab

400 g cooked shell-on prawns

400 g cooked brown shrimps

6 rock oysters

200 g cooked mussels

200 g cooked clams

200 g cooked whelks

100 g cooked shell-on razor clams

lemon wedges

garlic mayonnaise
(see page 169), to serve

Marie Rose sauce
(see page 166), to serve

Tabasco, to serve

Serves 2–4

This dish is perfect for shellfish lovers. Use the largest platter you can find and cover with crushed ice. Lay the seafood on top, and make sure you have plenty of lemon wedges, dips, picks and finger bowls to hand.

1 Arrange the crushed ice on the serving dish with a mound in the middle.

2 Cut the lobster in half, clean out the head and place in the centre of the plate. Remove the main body of the crab from the shell and remove the gills; remove the claws, crack with a swift hit of the rolling pin and cut the flesh from the main body of the crab into quarters. Place back in the shell and arrange the claws to look nice. Place in the centre of the platter.

3 Arrange the prawns on the ice. Do the same with the brown shrimps. Shuck the oysters and arrange around the edge of the dish. Remove the top shell from all the mussels, so the body remains in one side of the shell, and arrange in a pile on the dish. Scatter the remaining clams, whelks and razor clams here and there on the platter, ensuring they are evenly spread.

4 Serve the seafood platter in the centre of the table and give all the guests some lemon wedges and a small ramekin of each dip, together with a fork, pick and finger bowl. This will be very messy but it's worth the effort!

Note
You often find people are either lobster or crab lovers so a bit of trading can go on to make sure everybody gets a bit of what they love.

157

Kippers

Kippers (smoked herring), make a perfect luxury breakfast dish but, as with most things, you need to be very careful what you buy. Firstly, ask your fishmonger if they are smoked locally, as these will always be better than the vacuum-packed, mass-produced kippers you find in supermarkets. Each smokery will have its own way of smoking the fish, resulting in subtle differences.

4 x 200-g kippers

100 g butter

1 teaspoon chopped parsley

freshly toasted granary bread, to serve

Serves 4

1 Fill a frying pan with water and bring to a rolling boil. Immerse the whole kippers skin side down and poach for 10 minutes.

2 Remove from the pan and put on a plate, with a knob of butter melting on each. Sprinkle with a little chopped parsley and serve with hot buttered granary toast.

Kedgeree

olive oil, for frying

25 g unsalted butter

1 onion, finely chopped

300 g basmati rice

300 ml fish stock (see page 33)

100 ml milk

1 x 600-g cooked smoked haddock or pollock fillet, flaked

2 hard-boiled eggs, quartered

cayenne pepper, to serve

For the spice mix

1 teaspoon coriander seeds

1 teaspoon cumin seeds

1 teaspoon turmeric

1 teaspoon cayenne pepper

Serves 2

This popular breakfast dish is said to have been taken to India by Scottish troops, where it was spiced and then re-imported back to the United Kingdom. It remains a firm favourite and many different versions exist.

1 First make the spice mix. Warm a frying pan and add the coriander and cumin seeds and warm through for about 1 minute, until you get an intensely fragrant, slightly nutty aroma. If they start to burn throw them away and start again, cooking for a shorter time. Remove from the heat and place in a food processor with the remaining mix ingredients. Process until you have a fine powder.

2 Heat a little olive oil with the butter in the frying pan and cook the onion gently until soft. Add the basmati rice and allow it to absorb the oil. Then add a small amount of the fish stock, just enough to cover the rice and allow it to be absorbed. Add the spice mix and keep adding fish stock until the rice is cooked – this should take about 10 minutes. Add the milk and the fish. Cook through for a few minutes, stirring gently, but without breaking up the fish flakes. Finally add the boiled eggs cut into quarters and warm through.

3 Serve in a bowl with the cayenne pepper sprinkled on top.

Grilled North Atlantic langoustines

1 packet frozen langoustines
(16–18 langoustines)

50 g butter, softened

mixed fresh summer herbs
(parsley, basil, coriander, chives,
chervil)

lemon wedges, to serve

Serves 2

Langoustines are a good example of how our seafood tastes have changed in the last decades. Caught only in the North Atlantic, these cousins of the lobster have been cooked, peeled, coated in breadcrumbs, frozen and served up as scampi for decades. Yet in the last few years Scottish fishermen using small day boats have taken on the task of showing us what we have been missing by catching large langoustines sustainably, boxing them and shipping them live to high-class restaurants around the world.

1 Most langoustines are sold frozen in packs of 16 and this is what most fishmongers will be able to supply. Langoustines can handle being cooked and frozen better than most so in this rare instance this is an acceptable and affordable alternative. Thaw the frozen langoustines overnight in the fridge.

2 Once thawed split the langoustines down the middle with a sharp knife. Place on a baking tray. Finely chop the herbs and mix with the butter to make a herb butter. Cut into small knobs and place on the white meat of each langoustine. Place under a very hot grill for 5 minutes, until the butter melts and the edges of the shell start to brown. Remove from the grill and pile on a large plate. Serve with some lemon wedges and finger bowls as it can get quite messy.

Sole meunière

2 x 600-g Dover sole

100 g unsalted butter

1 bunch parsley, finely chopped

juice of 1 lemon

dash of white wine (optional)

salt and freshly ground black pepper

Serves 2

Dover sole is best served simply, so nothing interferes with its subtle flavour. Sole meunière is a classic recipe.

1 If not already done, cut the fins from the side, tail and around the edge of the fish. If the fish has not been skinned then simply place a small cut across the tail. Put some salt on your fingertips to get grip and pull towards the head. The skin should come off in one piece. Repeat on the other side.

2 Preheat the oven to 180°C/350°F/gas 4. Put the Dover sole on a baking tray lined with greaseproof paper, season and cook for 10 minutes. Remove the fish from the oven and check if it is cooked through. Melt the butter in a frying pan, add the parsley and lemon juice (you can add of dash of white wine at this point as well). Remove from the heat and pour over the sole to serve.

Oven-baked turbot with braised peas, bacon and baby onions

1 x 500-g tranche turbot

olive oil, for greasing

salt and freshly ground black pepper

For the peas

2 tablespoons olive oil

4 back bacon rashers, chopped

300 g frozen peas

juice of ½ lemon

250 g baby silverskin onions

salt and freshly ground black pepper

Serves 2

A turbot can vary in size from 600 g to 3–4 kg. They are a slow-growing fish so should only be bought when 30 cm or larger as they then will have had a chance to spawn a couple of times.

1 Preheat the oven to 200°C/400°F/gas 6. Line a baking tray with greaseproof paper and lightly oil the surface.

2 A tranche is simply a cut from the spine out across the flat wing of the fish. Ask your fishmonger to do this, as the spine is quite thick and finding the correct spot to start the cut can be difficult.

3 Season the turbot and place on the baking tray in the preheated oven for 20 minutes. Remove the turbot and look at the spine: the flesh should be just starting to go from pale to white. If it looks under-done then return to the oven for a few more minutes.

4 Make the peas. Heat the olive oil in a saucepan and fry the bacon rashers until golden brown. Add the peas and onions and cook until tender, about 5 minutes. Remove from the heat and squeeze over the lemon juice and season to taste.

5 Place a couple of ladlefuls of the braised peas in a bowl, lay the trance of turbot on top and serve.

Sauces, side dishes & desserts

Tartare sauce

150 ml mayonnaise
(see page 169)

1 tablespoon capers,
finely chopped

1 tablespoon gherkins,
finely chopped

1 tablespoon finely chopped
flat-leaf parsley

1 shallot, finely diced

juice of 1 lemon

salt and freshly ground black
pepper

A classic accompaniment to most fish dishes. Homemade
tartare sauce is greatly superior to shop-bought.

1 Mix all the ingredients together in a bowl then season to taste with
salt and pepper. Store in an airtight container in the fridge.

Marie Rose sauce

300 ml mayonnaise
(see page 169)

75 g ketchup

30 ml brandy

2 teaspoons Worcestershire sauce

juice of 1 lemon

½ teaspoon cayenne pepper

salt and freshly ground black
pepper

An essential sauce to serve with seafood and the basis of
prawn cocktail (see page 76). It is easy and quick to make
your own, and will always taste better than the shop-
bought variety.

1 Mix all the ingredients together in a bowl then season to taste with
salt and pepper. Store in an airtight container in the fridge.

Lemon crème fraîche

juice and grated rind of 2 lemons
300 ml crème fraîche

This lemon-flavoured crème fraîche is a perfect dipping sauce for a variety of fish and seafood dishes. It can also be served over a number of desserts.

1 Mix the lemon juice and rind with the crème fraîche and chill in the fridge in an airtight container. This will keep for 5 days.

Horseradish sour cream

100 g fresh horseradish
300 ml sour cream
white pepper

Simple and quick to prepare, this horseradish-flavoured sour cream is the perfect partner for smoked salmon. Try it spread on blinis and topped with a spoonful of caviar or lumpfish roe.

1 Grate the horseradish on the fine side of the grater and mix into the sour cream. Season with white pepper, mix well and store in the fridge in an airtight container.

Mayonnaise

2 egg yolks

1 tablespoon white wine vinegar

1 teaspoon Dijon mustard

juice of ½ lemon

290 ml vegetable oil

salt and freshly ground black pepper

No cook should ignore proper, homemade mayonnaise. Never add the oil too quickly or the mixture will separate. You can flavour the finished product with any number of ingredients to taste, such as garlic (see below), a herb of your choice, anchovies or even blue cheese.

1 Put the egg yolks in a food processor then add the white wine vinegar, some salt and pepper, mustard and lemon juice. Process to mix then, with the motor running, slowly and gradually trickle in the oil until the mixture starts to thicken. When all the oil has been added correct the seasoning if necessary and thin the mayonnaise down if needed by adding a little cold water.

2 Store in the fridge in an airtight container and use within 5 days.

Garlic mayonnaise

Simply add 2 crushed garlic cloves to the food processor with the other ingredients and continue as above.

169

Citrus butter

250 g unsalted butter, softened

juice and grated rind of 1 lime

juice and grated rind of 1 lemon

juice and grated rind of 1 orange

pinch of freshly ground black pepper

Citrus fruit and fish were meant to go together. It is useful to keep some of this butter in the fridge – melt gently on top of simply grilled, fried or baked fish at the end of the cooking time to liven it up. This butter will keep for about a week in the fridge. You can also freeze it – just use a sharp knife to slice off what you need.

1 Cream the butter in a mixing bowl then add all the other ingredients and mix well. Scrape the butter out on to parchment paper, roll out into a long sausage shape and chill in the fridge.

Peppercorn butter

250 g unsalted butter, softened

35 g green peppercorns in brine, drained

35 g pink peppercorns in brine, drained

pinch of freshly ground black pepper

This strongly flavoured butter goes well with most fish dishes. It is also good melted over cooked meat.

1 Cream the butter in a mixing bowl. Put the peppercorns in a food processor and process to break them up slightly then add them to the butter mixture, along with the black pepper. Scrape the butter out on to parchment paper, roll out into a long sausage shape and chill in the fridge.

Garlic and herb butter

250 g unsalted butter, softened
6 garlic cloves garlic, puréed
½ bunch parsley, chopped
freshly ground black pepper

As with the citrus butter (see page 170), it is very handy to keep this in the fridge. It adds instant flavour to a variety of fish dishes, and can also be melted over cooked meat.

1 Cream the butter in a mixing bowl then add all the other ingredients and mix well. Scrape the butter out on to parchment paper, roll out into a long sausage shape and chill in the fridge.

Brown butter

35 g unsalted butter
2 teaspoons lemon juice
1 tablespoon capers
10 g tomatoes, skinned, deseeded and chopped
½ tablespoon chopped parsley

Brown butter is a classic accompaniment to pan-fried or grilled fish, typically skate wing. The butter is heated until it just starts to go brown, when it takes on a pleasing nutty flavour.

1 Heat the butter in a hot frying pan until it starts going nut brown. Add the lemon juice, capers, tomato and parsley then spoon the sauce over the fish.

172

Citrus salsa

2 tomatoes, skinned, deseeded and quartered

1 large red onion, finely diced

1 large red chilli, deseeded and finely diced

1 lime, peeled, the white pith removed and the flesh cut into small segments

1 orange, peeled, the white pith removed and the flesh cut into small segments

1 tablespoon caster sugar

1 tablespoon chopped coriander

Salsas are very popular and fresh-tasting. This citrus salsa packs quite a punch with the addition of the chilli and makes a lively accompaniment to fish.

1 Put all the ingredients in a bowl, mix together and set aside to infuse.

Salsa verde

6 tablespoons chopped flat-leaf parsley

2 tablespoons capers, chopped

1 garlic clove, crushed

4 anchovy fillets

30 g breadcrumbs

pinch of salt and freshly ground black pepper

juice of ½ lemon

5 tablespoons olive oil

This Italian sauce can be used over fish, or as a dipping sauce for seafood.

1 Place the parsley, capers, garlic, anchovies, breadcrumbs and salt and pepper in a food processor and process until puréed. Add the lemon juice and olive oil and process until smooth.

173

Sauce vierge

100 ml olive oil

1 shallot, finely diced

2 tomatoes, skinned, deseeded and diced

juice of 1 lemon

2 teaspoons capers, chopped

2 teaspoons chopped parsley

2 teaspoons chopped basil

2 teaspoons chopped tarragon

2 teaspoons chopped coriander

This fresh sauce has become something of a modern classic. Easy and quick to make, it adds elegance and interest to a variety of fish dishes.

1 Put the olive oil in a saucepan and heat slowly over a low heat. When the oil is warm add all the other ingredients and allow to infuse.

Tomato and chilli jam

3 red chillies, deseeded and finely chopped

700 g ripe tomatoes, chopped

4 garlic cloves, crushed

1x 5-cm piece root ginger, peeled and grated

400 g demerara sugar

110 ml red wine vinegar

This spicy sauce has quite a kick and can be used over fish, or as a dipping sauce for seafood.

1 Place all the ingredients in a non-metallic saucepan and slowly bring to a simmer. If you have a thermometer then the temperature should be no higher than 220°C. Reduce until the liquid has started to thicken. Set aside and allow to cool.

2 Transfer to a sterlized jar and keep in the fridge for up to two weeks.

Salad dressing

1 tablespoon Dijon mustard

1 tablespoon runny honey

salt and freshly ground black pepper, to taste

1 garlic clove, crushed

50 ml good-quality vinegar (balsamic or red wine)

225 ml vegetable oil

It is very useful to keep a container of this basic salad dressing in the fridge. It is quick and easy to make, and is guaranteed to liven up any salad instantly.

1 Put the mustard, honey, salt and pepper, garlic and the vinegar in a mixing bowl and whisk together. Slowly drizzle in the oil, whisking continuously until it emulsifies, then chill in an airtight container in the fridge.

Shallot vinaigrette

300 ml red wine vinegar

100 g soft brown sugar

300 g shallots, finely diced

This intensely flavoured salad dressing adds a touch of luxury to any salad. It is also good spooned over seafood, particularly freshly shucked oysters.

1 Heat the vinegar and sugar in a saucepan and when the sugar has dissolved remove from the heat and allow to cool. When cool add the shallots and store in an airtight jar.

Rouille

1 egg yolk
1 tablespoon Dijon mustard
pinch of salt
¼ teaspoon cayenne pepper
½ tablespoon tomato purée
50 ml groundnut oil
50 ml extra-virgin olive oil

This classic Provençal mixture, not unlike mayonnaise, is traditionally spooned over fish soup, notably *bouillabaisse*. It can also be used as a garnish for a variety of fish dishes.

1 Put the egg yolk, mustard, salt, cayenne pepper and tomato purée in a food processor. Process to mix until smooth. With the motor running, slowly and gradually trickle in both oils until the mixture starts to thicken.

Thai paste

1 teaspoon shrimp paste
1 x 4-cm piece galangal, peeled
1 x 4-cm piece root ginger, peeled
5 large garlic cloves, peeled
3 large shallots, peeled and sliced
1 tablespoon soft brown sugar
1 lemongrass stalk, chopped
4 large chillies, deseeded and chopped
1 bunch coriander
1 teaspoon ground cumin
1 teaspoon salt
1 teaspoon ground pepper
oil

Making your own Thai paste is preferable to buying it. This paste forms the basis of a number of Thai curry dishes, adding heat and a subtle flavour to them.

1 Place all the ingredients in a food processor and process, stopping to scrape the mixture down the sides of the bowl and adding a little oil to loosen it if needed. When smooth, transfer the mixture to a saucepan and cook over a medium heat to infuse the flavours. Remove from the heat and allow to cool before storing.

Mushy peas

2 tablespoons olive oil

1 bunch spring onions, chopped

500 g frozen peas

75 g unsalted butter

1 bunch mint, chopped

salt and freshly ground black pepper, to taste

Serves 4

The classic accompaniment to fish and chips. Tempting though it is to buy the tinned variety, it is much better to make your own mushy peas as they will simply taste better.

1 Put the olive oil in a saucepan, season the spring onions with a little salt and pepper and cook them until soft. Add the peas and cook until thawed and then remove from the heat. Add the butter and mint and then, using a hand blender, purée the peas until smooth.

177

SAUCES, SIDE DISHES & DESSERTS

Chickpea, ginger and beansprout salad

1 x 400-g tin chickpeas, rinsed

500 g beansprouts

1 x 2-cm piece root ginger, peeled and thickly sliced

1 bunch coriander, chopped

salt and freshly ground black pepper, to taste

Serves 4

A delicious, Asian-style salad which can be assembled in minutes, this makes a good accompaniment to any spicy fish dish.

1 Put all the ingredients in a large mixing bowl and mix to serve.

Chocolate and pecan brownies with crème anglaise

150 g dark chocolate

150 g unsalted butter

100 g pecans, smashed

3 eggs

225 g soft brown sugar

1 vanilla pod, split in half lengthways and the seeds scraped out

100 g plain flour, sifted

For the crème anglaise

250 ml double cream

250 ml semi-skimmed milk

1 vanilla pod, split in half lengthways and the seeds scraped out

6 egg yolks

90 g caster sugar

Serves 6

Chocolate brownies are a real favourite and a great way to end a meal. We serve these warm as a dessert but you could always leave these to cool and store them in an airtight container for another time. The crème anglaise is a wonderful alternative to cream or ice cream.

1 Preheat the oven to 180°C/350°F/gas 4.

2 Place the chocolate and butter in a heatproof bowl and set over a pan of just simmering water. Stir gently until the chocolate has melted. Remove from the heat and add the smashed pecans.

3 In another mixing bowl whisk the eggs, sugar and vanilla seeds until smooth then fold in the flour. Fold in the melted chocolate, taking care not to over-mix, and pour into a parchment-lined baking tray measuring 23 x 33 cm. Bake in the oven for 20–25 minutes.

4 To make the crème anglaise, pour the double cream and milk into a saucepan and add the vanilla pod and seeds. Heat gently – do not let it come to a boil.

5 In a mixing bowl whisk the egg yolks and the caster sugar until light and creamy. Strain the milk and cream, whisk into the egg yolk and sugar mixture then return to the pan and cook over a low heat, stirring continuously with a rubber spatula until the mixture starts to thicken (it should be the consistency of a light custard).

6 Remove the baking tray from the oven and allow to cool for a few minutes before turning out onto a cooling rack. Cut into squares and serve with the crème anglaise on the side.

Tarte au citron
with fruit coulis

1 packet ready-made shortcrust pastry

flour, for dusting

6 egg yolks

220 g caster sugar

juice and grated rind of 4 lemons

grated rind of 2 oranges

150 ml double cream

For the fruit coulis

100 g strawberries

100 g raspberries

50 ml cold water

50 g caster sugar

Serves 8 ·

A lemon tart rounds off a fish-based meal very successfully. The fruit sauce suggested here acts as the perfect partner.

1 Preheat the oven to 180°C/350°F/gas 4. Lightly grease a 23-cm loose-bottomed flan tin. Roll out the pastry on a lightly floured surface until you have a circle large enough to cover the tin. Press gently into the tin, prick the base with a fork and trim away any excess.

2 Line the pastry with non-stick baking paper and baking beans and bake 'blind' for about 10 minutes. Remove the beans and paper and return to the oven for a further 10 minutes. Remove and set aside to cool. Reduce the oven temperature to 140°C/275°F/gas 1.

3 Place the egg yolks and caster sugar in a mixing bowl and whisk together until light and creamy. Add the grated lemon rind and juice together with the grated orange rind and the double cream. Mix together and leave to settle. Skim off the bubbles and then pour the mixture into the pastry case and bake in the oven for about 30 minutes, until the mixture has a jelly-like wobble.

4 Make the coulis. Cut the strawberries in half and put them in a saucepan, together with the raspberries, water and sugar. Cook the fruit for about 5 minutes or until soft, then transfer to a food processor and blend until smooth. Push the coulis through a sieve before serving to ensure there are no pips in it. Serve with the warm tart.

Classic crème brûlée with shortbread

600 ml double cream

1 vanilla pod, split in half lengthways and the seeds scraped out

4 egg yolks

125 g caster sugar

2 tablespoons demerara sugar

For the shortbread

240 g unsalted butter, softened

120 g caster sugar

360 g plain flour

Serves 6

Crème brûlée is among the repertory of classic desserts and is universally liked. Serve simply, with shortbread.

1 Pour the double cream into a saucepan, add the vanilla pod and seeds and heat slowly – do not let it come to a boil. Whisk the egg yolk and caster sugar together until light and creamy then mix in the warmed cream. Return to the pan and cook over a low heat, stirring continuously with a rubber spatula until thick.

2 Divide among ramekins and chill in the refrigerator for about 30 minutes. Sprinkle the top of each ramekin with demerara sugar and and use a mini blow torch on them so the sugar topping caramelizes. Alternatively you can place them under a very hot grill for a few seconds. Chill in the fridge until the topping hardens.

3 Make the shortbread. Preheat the oven to 175°C/350°F/gas 4. Cream the butter in a mixing bowl then mix in the sugar and flour until the mixture is smooth. Wrap the mixture tightly in a double layer of cling film and chill in the fridge.

4 When firm, roll out the pastry on a board until 1 cm thick. Cut into circles or a rectangle and place on a baking tray lined with greaseproof paper. Cook in the oven for about 10–12 minutes. Serve the shortbread with the chilled crème brûlée.

183

Pear tarte tatin with vanilla mascarpone

6 pears, peeled and quartered

85 g unsalted butter

100 g caster sugar

10 ml cold water

1 teaspoon ground cinnamon

250 g puff pastry, rolled out into a circle

For the sugar syrup

1.2 litres water

1 cinnamon stick

2 cloves

250 g caster sugar

grated rind of 1 lemon

1 star anise

For the vanilla mascarpone

2 vanilla pods, split in half lengthways and the seeds scraped out

250 g mascarpone

Serves 6

A variation on the classic tarte tatin, which is made with apples, this makes an elegant dessert served with vanilla-flavoured mascarpone instead of cream.

1 First make the sugar syrup. Pour the water into a saucepan and add all the other ingredients. Stir until the sugar has dissolved. Preheat the oven to 200°C/400°F/gas 6.

2 Lightly poach the pears in the sugar syrup for about 10 minutes, or until soft, then remove and allow to cool. Heat the butter, sugar, cold water and cinnamon in a circular flameproof pan that will also go in the oven until caramelized then remove and allow to cool slightly.

3 Place the pear quarters in a circle pattern around the pan then place the puff pastry on top. Tuck the pastry neatly around the edges and place in the oven. After about 15 minutes reduce the oven temperature to 180°C/350°F/gas 4 and cook for a further 10 minutes, or until golden brown.

4 Make the mascarpone. Add the vanilla seeds (reserve the pods for another use) to the mascarpone and mix together well. Chill in the fridge. This will keep in the fridge for 7 days.

5 Remove the tarte tatin from the oven and turn over onto a serving plate, so the pears are uppermost. Arrange the pears more neatly while the tart is still warm and the caramel hasn't fully set. Serve with the vanilla mascarpone.

When fish are in season

Jan Feb Mar Apr May Jun Jul Aug Sep Oct Nov Dec

Bream (wild)
Brill
Clams
Cockles
Cod
Cornish sardines
Crab
Dover sole
Farmed mussels
Gurnard (pink and grey)
Hake
Herring
Huss/dogfish
John Dory
Lemon sole
Lobster
Mackerel
Monkfish
Mullet (grey)
Mullet (red)
Oysters (native)
Oysters (rock)
Plaice
Pollock
Prawns
Scallops
Sea bass (wild)
Skate
Squid
Triggerfish
Turbot
Whelks
Whiting

These are only rough guides as fish and shellfish move around according to the
temperature of the sea and how rough it is. Always ask your local fishmonger for advice.

Index

Acknowledgements

It never takes just a few people to write a cookbook. There is a whole team of people who worked feverishly to put this together, but it would never have happened if Clare Sayer from New Holland Publishers had not sent a little email asking if we would be interested in doing a book. So the credit for this must go to Clare and her team at New Holland for instigating it. Then there are the food shots. Loz and I turned up at a studio in central London first thing one Thursday morning, dragging a coolbox full of the best-looking fish we could find. Tony Briscoe really made the recipes come alive along with Claire Greenstreet's amazing food styling. Geoff Borin also did a great job putting together such a fantastic design.

Fishy Fishy would be nothing without the hard and dangerous work that fishermen do everyday – hopefully we conveyed that with the piece on cod fishing that featured Gary Brownrigg and Peter Budden, who allowed us onto the Catherine Ann to show how our cod is caught. Matt and Jane Leach at Brighton and Newhaven Fish Sales have also supported us from the beginning and Jane's FISH fishmongers is probably the best in Sussex – if not the south of England – so thank you to them.

On a business note we would still be sitting around that dinner table talking about Fishy Fishy if it was not for James Gallimore and his team at Atlantic Swiss who believed in what we were trying to do and helped make it happen. They introduced us to Robert Johnson, whose talents as an editor came in handy when he looked through the first draft of the book, and Annabel Moorsom from Sorted PA. We also would not have the wonderful genius that is Charlotte Hickson from Monsta and her team who have worked tirelessly to keep us in the limelight.

In putting the book together we tapped into all parts of the Fishy Fishy family. Jonathon Kemp's recipe for potato salad was a no-brainer. Geoff Pugh happily spent a cold day taking some publicity shots for us and of course we must thank the wonderful Hazel Thompson, who took a break from award-winning documentary reportage to spend two days on a rocking boat taking pictures of cod and all of us fishing for mackerel. Thank you as well to the group who were forced to knock back large quantities of white wine and lobster for the lobsterfest feature and to all our families and friends who have eaten more fish in the last year than they probably have in their lifetime.

Finally, and probably most importantly, thanks to Loz Talent, our head chef and fish lover through and through, for all those hours we sat in front a computer trying to work out portion sizes. To all our staff at the restaurants, thanks for all your hard work. And to Dee Koppang, Dermot O'Leary, Alice Rivers Cripps: well done, we did it!

James and Paul

PS Thank you to all our Fishy Fishy customers – we look forward to continuing to serve you the best fresh, local and seasonal fish and seafood.